Reporting For Television

REPORTING
FOR
TELEVISION

Carolyn Diana Lewis

New York • Columbia University Press • 1984

Library of Congress Cataloging in Publication Data

Lewis, Carolyn.
    Reporting for television.

    Includes index.
    1. Television broadcasting of news.
2. Reporters and reporting.   I. Title.
PN4784.T4L4   1983   070.1'9   83-7568
ISBN 0-231-05538-2

Photographs are courtesy of Kenneth Tiven, News Director, WPXI, Pittsburgh. *Photographer:* Michael Parker

Columbia University Press
New York   Guildford, Surrey

*Clothbound editions of Columbia University Press books are Smyth-sewn
and printed on permanent and durable acid-free paper.*

To my sons,
Peter and David

Contents

Illustrations appear in two groups: After pp. 63 and 109

Preface

Reporting for Television is intended as a practical manual for students of broadcast reporting and for new reporters and producers at local television stations. It is an effort to combine instruction on the nuts-and-bolts of field reporting with some theories and practices in the reporting process.

The book grew out of my early work as a teacher of broadcast journalism, first at Boston University, and later at Columbia University's Graduate School of Journalism. I came to teaching after a long career in print, radio, and television journalism, and like many professionals-turned-instructor I thought that the transition would be an easy one.

I discovered instead that there is a considerable difference between knowing how to practice reporting and knowing how to explain those practices to students. I was confronted with the need to find the logic, principles, and system in the way that I and other reporters gathered information, evaluated it, and translated it into the television medium. Much of what I had learned on the job was by now instinctual, which is all right for the practicing professional, but singularly unhelpful when teaching students.

As a result, I was led to study and analyze the way that the television reporter operates, and then to break the techniques into components that could be transmitted to my students.

My goals as a teacher were several: to offer practical instruction in the field reporting and packaging process, to explain the reporter's mindset and some of the techniques he employs to obtain and evaluate information, and to draw a comparison between the news as it is and how it might be.

It was my intention to lead students through the labyrinth of journalistic and technological challenges they are likely to encounter as a working reporter. I began by making outlines, jotting down notes, and developing material that grew out of common questions and problems that emerged from lecture classes and field reporting experiences.

What surprised me at first was the general ignorance of both undergraduate and graduate students of how the news business works. I found that I could presume very little in the way of knowledge and understanding of subjects like "what is news" and "the differences between print and broadcasting."

In addition, while I found that I could lay out general reporting principles, each story covered by a student was both specific and specifically different. The student had to find a way to take the general principles and apply them flexibly, creatively, and intelligently to ever-varying events and subject matter. As a result, the classroom and field instruction constituted only two-thirds of the teaching process. The final portion occurred in the specific criticism and evaluation that followed completion of each student's news project.

So much of good television reporting depends upon the reporter's education, sensitivity, and good judgment that I found myself regularly confounded by the difficulty of teaching a higher level of television journalism to undergraduates and graduates at Boston University, and to graduates at Columbia. The mechanics could be taught, of course; but how do you teach thought-processes, analytical skills, and the art of writing vividly and masterfully? Especially, how do you teach these in a short span of time, when so much of student energy is directed toward mastering the complexity of the technology?

Much of the instruction at the Columbia Graduate School of Journalism involves learning by doing. In a program that is only nine months long, it is necessary to impose long working hours, plus the tight deadlines and the disciplines of a professional news organization, even as the careful teaching proceeds. In the television workshop, as indeed in other areas of the curriculum that are nonbroadcast, the individual teacher is constantly trying to teach substance along with technique. Furthermore, since the practice of journalism is at best an inexact science, highly individualistic and open to sundry variations, the teacher has to explore the yins and the yangs of every story, instead of stating categorically that "this is the way it is." There is very little room for dogma in journalism or the teaching of journalism.

I realize that the teaching of substance has to be interwoven with the daily process of news coverage. What substance is taught will depend upon the nature of the story covered by the student and the questions raised by the story. I have designed a book which deals in only a minor way with the substance of journalism—history, politics, economics, science, sociology, and so forth. I believe that it is beyond the reach of any one teacher or any one book to incorporate so wide a field. What I have chosen to do instead is relatively narrow and practical: to make the connection between a textbook and the real world.

With that practicality in mind, I decided to write a book that would prepare a student for local, not network television. Students who graduate from journalism programs generally do not find their first jobs at networks, but at local commercial stations where the journalistic and economic imperatives are different from those that operate at the networks.

In writing this book, I am afraid that I have made public some of my personal ambivalence toward the local news product. I believe that local news can rise to extraordinary heights and at the same time it can be awful. It can be silly and tawdry, but it can also be magnificent. Its definition of news normally fails to match the definitions common to established newspapers and networks, and yet it often reveals and defines the life of a community in ways that traditional news operations do not. It is a curious, perplexing animal, still searching both for its soul and for its ethic.

My purpose in writing this book is to help the teacher of journalism or the news director who is training newly employed reporters to prepare the neophyte reporter for the existing reality of local news. At the same time, I have shared some of my professional values, developed over the twenty years that I worked as a reporter. I am certain that there can and will be arguments over some of the reporting principles that I espouse. I find that prospect perfectly appropriate in a profession which tends to spurn rigid rules and definitions and is by its nature cheerfully contentious.

While I hope that this book will help in the instruction of techniques, it will also inspire discussion and debate on how news is gathered and presented and how local television news can be made better than it is. As I will indicate, the quality of the news product is determined by the demands of the medium, the economic imperatives of the local television news business, and other factors, many of them nonjournalistic in nature. The hope that lurks deep in the heart of many teachers, myself included, is that some-how their students will go out and make it better. However, before anyone can do that, he should understand why local television news is the way it is, and what it demands *now* of its reporters, producers, and management.

Acknowledgments

This book would never have been written if not for the enthusiasm and encouragement of a former student at Columbia, Mark Levine. Mark was in his mid-thirties, and a lawyer, when he became a student in my broadcast journalism class. It was he who suggested that my assorted notes and written instructions might be turned into a book. Subsequently, Mark established his own one-man publishing house, Scarf Press, and became the agent for my book. My thanks go to him for his patience and his help during the many months that I struggled with the book, while I was also juggling my teaching and administrative duties at the Columbia Journalism School.

My thanks, too, to my boss, Dean Osborn Elliott, for his encouragement, his good humor, and his help, during the long months when his offsider worked and worried over her manuscript. As a former editor-in-chief at *Newsweek*, Dean Elliott is plainly a print journalist. However, he has shown by his interest in and commitment to the broadcast journalism program at the Journalism School that he perceives television news as a serious and worthy enterprise.

My thanks to Janet West Abrams, my former secretary who is now assistant director of the Alfred I. DuPont—Columbia Broadcast Journalism Awards program; and my former assistant, Doreen Forney, for their cheerful and willing help in typing the rough draft of the manuscript.

Finally, I want to thank Kenneth Tiven, news director at WPXI, Channel 11, in Pittsburgh, for his patient and detailed reading, editing, and critique of my chapters and for providing photographs for this book. Ken and I go back a long way. When I was a reporter at station WTOP in Washington, D.C., Ken was executive producer. In the months and years that I worked with him, I came to respect his honesty, integrity, and dedication to the highest values of journalism. He was and is a pragmatist. He recognizes the limitations as well as the possibilities of the medium. He concedes that if a news operation is to survive, it must attract the mass of viewers and hold their attention. However, I have never known him to compromise his principles, or to forget that he is a journalist first and a television person second.

When I needed to find someone in the business of local television news whose wisdom, judgment, and values I could trust and respect, I naturally and comfortably turned to Ken. The fact that he found time to read through the manuscript and to make some significant interpolations, suggestions, and edits at a time when he was also running his Pittsburgh news operation and building new studios there is a testament to his generosity of spirit.

For all his help and guidance, I thank him. However any errors of judgment or fact within the book are my responsibility alone.

Carolyn Diana Lewis
August 1983

Reporting For Television

CHAPTER ONE.

Print Reporting Versus Reporting for Television

Broadcast journalism is first and foremost journalism. It deals in fact, not fiction, and it requires the same diligence and the same dedication to accuracy, fairness, and balance that underpin journalism in the print medium.

Yet plainly broadcast journalism is different from print journalism, too. Robyn Smith retains a small measure of anonymity if she has a newspaper byline. It is only her name that goes public. On television, however, she is both seen and heard. Her involvement is perceived as personal and direct, and her identification with the story is difficult to separate from the story itself.

If the television reporter's "personality" intrudes on the event being covered, then the technology of television is not far behind. We all know how an individual will purposefully put his best smile forward when a friend or a relative turns a still camera in his direction. Most news sources can be expected to behave with the same self-consciousness when confronted with a television camera. The television reporter can thus find it hard to capture reality or truth, when the image that the news source consciously projects is a contrived and self-flattering one.

Print reporters, who record information with pad and pencil, are aware that some sources are easily intimidated by the realization that their every word is being engraved in the reporter's notebook. In time, the individual may be persuaded to forget the pad and pencil, but it is harder to ignore a camera.

Clearly, the nature of the television medium demands that the broadcast reporter develop knowledge and skills that go beyond the basic and immutable ones required of print reporters. He must understand the demands and the quirks of the medium, the limits and possibilities of the technology, and even more, he has to understand the effect of the news-gathering process on the people who are the objects of his reports.

The modern politician tends to be media-wise. The smarter ones have learned how to use television as a means to promote themselves and their ideas. The television reporter can either allow himself to be used as a passive conduit to the public, or he can learn how to "play his fish on the line," using the interplay between the politician and the camera in a way that will serve to *reveal* reality rather than mask it.

Ordinary citizens, too, can be media wise—or else struck dumb. They can hype their comments in order to win access to the airwaves, or they can be awed and intimidated by the camera, fearful that they may reveal themselves in unplanned and unexpected ways. The television reporter needs to be especially alert to citizen-manipulation, on the one hand, and he has to learn how to put the nervous citizen at ease, on the other.

A major part of the reporter's job is to lead the news subject to the point where he can express his true feelings, as though the camera were not there at all.

When that happens, the television camera becomes an instrument of wonderful revelation, peeling away the outer masks, and catching what might otherwise be missed. A memorable example of this phenomenon occurred in a late-seventies interview of Senator Edward Kennedy by then-CBS correspondent Roger Mudd. The Senator was plainly intending to embark on a campaign for the Presidential nomination, but when Mudd asked him why he wanted to be President, Kennedy appeared to be struck dumb, as though he had never seriously entertained the question. It was not so much the words that were spoken as it was the physical and emotional reaction to the questions that revealed the Senator's confusion. Television news is replete with memorable occasions like this one, testifying to its power to lay bare realities that are sometimes difficult to translate into the printed word.

The television reporter must learn how to make the technology the servant of his journalism, not its master. Before he can feel in control of his story; before he can free his time and energies for the difficult job of getting the facts, evaluating them, and shaping them into a meaningful story; before he can do any of this successfully, he has to understand the technology and how it interacts with human beings.

Stung by the growing success and power of television as a news vehicle, some print reporters have taken to pooh-poohing broadcast journalism, damning it as "showbiz" or shallow. They will point to the brevity of the news on television, and say—quite rightly as it happens—that twenty-two minutes on CBS can hardly compare with the mighty solemnities of *The New York Times*.

However, it is impossible to equate space in print with time on air. It is plain that a lengthy story in a magazine or a newspaper provides more depth and complexity than almost anything seen on television, including the best of documentaries. But the measuring rods used in this comparison are almost always determined by people in the print medium. They choose to measure television news according to what print does best, and thus they find television wanting. By defining the issues in print terms, and excluding values in which television excels, they skew the results. It is as if scientists chose to damn the medium of printed words because some advanced mathematical formulas can be better explained by numbers.

Each medium has its own strengths and weaknesses, its particular usefulness and value in the scheme of things. To convey certain realities, print, too, can be an imperfect vehicle, especially in the hands of the more plodding practitioners of the writing trade. Yet it is the medium we turn to most for background, history, context, and explanation, and so we should.

Ideally, television news—impressionistic and brief as it is—never could become a substitute for reading. Television can attract the attention, stir the emotions, dress up abstractions in human attire, personalize broad issues, reveal character, and give viewers the sense of having participated in an event. Nevertheless, citizens ought to know more about their complex and dangerous surroundings than can be offered by so ephemeral and epigrammatic a medium.

Unfortunately, the trend is in the other direction. On August 8, 1982, *The New York Times* reported that 64 percent of Americans now rely on television as their primary source of news. In their book *Remote Control* (Quadrangle, 1978) Frank Mankiewicz and Joel Swerdlow report that the average American is spending less and less time with his daily newspaper. In fact he reads his newspaper for no more than one half-hour each day. Furthermore, they say, "This decline holds true for all economic, educational and age groupings. While the amount of television viewing is constantly increasing, the gap between amount of viewing by the well educated and the poorly educated is narrowing."

In sum, the public likes television. And indeed, many of the individuals who now watch television news would never have bought a newspaper in the first place. At least these people are being exposed to some news of the world around them. There is also evidence that a good television news story can inspire sufficient interest to lead the viewer to read more about the subject. One of the beneficiaries of this interest has been the weekly newsmagazine.

The challenge to the broadcast reporter is to offer to this vast and growing television audience as much quality information as the medium will allow. It is his job to tell the news in such a way that it attracts and holds the attention, that it informs honestly and intelligently, and that it leaves the viewer with fresh understanding, however limited. Even more, a good television news story can encourage the viewer to care about the issues and the people involved in the stories.

In spite of its obvious and built-in limitations, news transmitted through the television medium offers a quality of communication that is beyond the capability of the print medium. The printed word becomes meaningful to the reader only when the reader connects his private mind-picture to the intent of the writer. The reader surveys the words, translates them into mental pictures, and then creates his meanings out of that.

Television simplifies the process. The picture is there on the screen: all that the viewer has to do is impose his inner meaning on the image, or the combination of spoken word and image. Instead of going from written word-to-picture-to-meaning, his mind travels directly from picture-to-meaning.

In neither case can we be sure that the viewer or reader captures the meaning as it was first intended by the communicator, since each of us absorbs information according to our individual history and receptivity. But perhaps television is more beguiling to growing numbers of citizens, because it offers a less cumbersome, more direct, and natural means of communicating.

Long before *Homo sapiens* learned to scribble on tablets, he employed the spectacle of ceremony and the spoken language of the storyteller to communicate with his fellow tribesmen. This had obvious limitations for the advancement of civilization, since there was no way to transmit knowledge from one generation to another except by word of mouth, and the transmission was limited by the need for geographic proximity. However, the exercise did embrace a certain warmth and charm. Instead of reading a lengthy written description of how the medicine man doffed his feather hat and danced about the ring, early man could see the event for himself. Instead of reading a written excerpt indicating the words that the medicine man intoned, he could hear the actual words as they were spoken, watch the manner in which they were spoken, and judge for himself whether the magic had the power to work.

Television news offers much of the same verity, although in truncated form. Neither print nor videotape can substitute for the reality of the event itself, and both media forms reshape the reality when the reporter selectively chooses what will go into the news report and what will be left out. Nevertheless, a comparison between a direct quote in print and the film or videotape of the speaker speaking those same words, shows that in fact television offers more information, and in a less ambiguous form.

The television viewer receives the words, but in addition, he can hear the intonation and the timbre of the voice, watch the expression of the eyes, notice the turn of the chin and the shrug of the shoulder, in short, partake of the subtle insinuations of face and body language. What is available to the viewer is a measure of the sincerity behind the words: in the *way* that the news source speaks, he often can reveal himself.

Critics who complain that television news suffers from brevity, and who merely count the seconds on the air, fail to take account of the fact that television is operating on two levels at once: the verbal and the visual. Senator X may be speaking only one brief line on television, while he is quoted in many lines in the printed newspaper story. But on television, Senator X offers his whole self, not merely his words as recorded by a print reporter. Even when the television reporter is relating part of the story in his own words delivered "voice-over" pictures, information is imparted on two levels. The viewer sees and the viewer hears: it is a form of communication that differs from reading, but is not necessarily less useful or less valid, in terms of human understanding.

Another way that television reporting differs from print is revealed by the common saying in television news that "you only go around once." That means the story has to be told in a way that is clear and simple because the viewer does not get a second chance to see it.

By contrast, a print story can be reread. An idea missed the first time can be reexamined. How many readers bother to reread a difficult story it is hard to tell, but newspapers have traditionally put the meat of their stories in headlines and first paragraphs on the presumption that most readers fail to read beyond that.

What the newspaper does offer is a choice. The reader can, if he chooses, read some parts of the paper, and ignore the rest. He can read this part now and that part later. He can read one story in depth and skim another.

Television, however, offers information that is delivered at a specific time. It is watched from the top on down, in sequential order, without catering to the individual viewer's personal interests. The newspaper reader may not like a particular story or idea that is in his paper, but his distaste for a single item is unlikely to cause him to toss the paper into the fireplace and cancel his subscription on the spot. He simply skips that story and turns to the part of the newspaper that interests and pleases him.

The television viewer cannot pick and choose items within the news broadcast, but he has a simple weapon to drive an unwanted face or idea from his screen: he can change the channel.

This freedom to switch midstream accounts in part for the apparent showiness and shrillness of much television news. Each news report is designed to grab the attention of the viewer, and to hold it tight, or else almost all is lost. If the viewer changes channels, what is lost is not just that one story, but possibly the entire program, and with it the program's ratings and the advertiser's dollars.

While the print reporter is conscious that he should be writing bright and grabby news leads and that his copy should be clear and well-written, he does not have the feeling that the entire newspaper enterprise rests on his solitary talents. However, in television news, the prevailing ethos is that one slip, one miss, will lead the viewer to that Other Station, from whence he will never return. As a result, television reporters are encouraged to employ almost any means to make a story so arresting that millions of viewers will be frozen in their seats, too enthralled to flick to another channel.

These economic imperatives, and the culture that they create in television newsrooms, produce internal conflicts with traditional ideas of journalism. For example, if a public official is a dull man, but what he has to say is important, the dullness of his delivery is not very likely to affect the length or character of a print story. By means of explanatory paragraphs and inter-polations, and by use of artful paraphrasing, the meaning of the official's words can be communicated in print. But in television, where the viewer is likely to be bored by a dull presentation, the reporter is inclined to use very little of that particular sound-bite or quotation on the air. The temptation is to edit out the final words of the official's statement, even if they happen to qualify significantly what he is trying to impart. Furthermore, if he is an abysmal speaker, he may never get on the air at all.

What is in opposition here is the need to fairly report important state-ments and the subtleties of someone's meanings, as against the supposed requirement never to bore the audience. Where meaning is sacrificed to the never-bore-the-audience god, news executives will argue that there is no point in plunging ahead with dull material if the viewer is going to switch it off anyhow.

Having said that, television newsmen point out that the print medium has its flaws and its limits, too. For one thing, existing newspaper technol-ogy delivers the news some time after an event has taken place. Thus the information you read in your morning paper may no longer be correct or up-to-date. Furthermore, print reporters will themselves acknowledge that the visual impact of videotape and the immediacy of television deliver a news product that is livelier and more vital than almost anything possible in print.

The point here is that each of the media has its strengths and weaknesses, and each has its particular value to the consumer of news. Furthermore, in its own way, each has to struggle with the imperatives of profit-making in a public service form of enterprise. Whatever the medium, the idealism of reporters and producers is bound to be tempered by the realities of dead-lines, the character of management, projected audience, competition, and the bottom line, as well as the nature of the medium itself. The charge is to do the best one can with the materials at hand.

The goal of the neophyte television reporter, then, is to learn how to do what has to be done in the best way humanly and technologically possible, in order to better serve the public. If at times she finds herself frustrated by the medium's limitations, she should know that any form of journalism has its frustrations. Any form of journalism will fall short of the larger reality it reports about. However, before Robyn Smith can expect to lead a private revolution to change or improve the way that a particular medium covers news, she had best learn to master the basic skills and comprehend the various forces that make the medium operate the way it does.

For example, in television, the *spoken* word is king, and that is a different form of communication than the printed word. The student who is still in college, or the newly employed reporter fresh from academe, will probably have to struggle to slough off the tedious, turgid, and tangled perambulations that won him A's in social studies or in philosophy classes. Language that is designed to impress, either by its length or the obscurity of its formulations, is bad enough in printed form, but in television news, it is fatal.

The fact is, we do not speak the way we write, and it's a good thing, too. Something seems to happen to many people when they sit down with a pen or at a typewriter. They grow formal or pompous; their reasoning becomes circuitous and opaque. Perhaps it is a sense that putting something down on paper is permanent, that this treatise is for posterity and therefore it had better be filled with fine, multisyllabic words and erudite sentiments. When we speak—except maybe when we are addressing large audiences—we tend to speak to each other casually and informally. There is a certain simple grace, a directness that helps, rather than hinders, communication.

Writing for television is writing for speaking. You tell a story, like the old shaman told his story way back before tablets were invented. The language may not be quite so informal as the slap-you-on-the-back and hey-man lingo of the streets, but it should be lean and uncluttered and *speak*-able.

Because television requires brevity, it forces the reporter to produce crisp, direct prose, to tell the story in a personal and conversational manner, without the long-winded subterfuges often used to cover up muddy thinking on paper. Broadcast writing is precision writing. It is lean verbal art melded with technical visual skill. The reporter has to learn to grab onto the essence of a story, go straight to the meat of it, and to strike in as few words as possible. Often he has to write "to time"—that is, write precisely twenty seconds or twenty-three seconds of copy—and not one whit more or less.

What television writing teaches is that it is more useful to tell a few essential facts about a news story, to tell them vividly and well, than it is to ramble hither and thither, touching on everything and leaving confusion. A good television writer can find the exact one word or phrase that is pithy and pointed. Combined with fine pictures and eloquent sound, that's mighty powerful stuff.

The operating principle is simple: Do not try to tell everything. Accept that in television news there are limits, and the sternest limit is time. Search for moments of truth, sparkling vignettes, compressed illustrations of fact, small parts of a larger reality. Spurn the cosmic, and instead focus precisely on one or two elements of a story.

That judgment has to be made swiftly, on the scene, even as the story is unfolding. Which pictures to shoot, what not to shoot, whom to interview, which facts are central—all of these decisions have to be made on the spot. Because of these imperatives, good television journalism requires a finely honed news sense. Unlike the newspaper reporter, Robyn Smith will rarely have the luxury of talking over the story with her editor, or writing the story after recent coverage of an in-progress event. Her deadlines are immediate. She has to get the pictures now—or never. Television journalism has a seat-of-the-pants quality that requires vital news judgments to be made instantaneously in the field and in the control room.

For anyone who is serious about the news business, it is important to be informed. The reporter needs to develop the habit of reading newspapers thoroughly, and reading not like an ordinary citizen but like a professional. The reporter should read not only what happens to interest him, but everything, and he should read it carefully with the thought that any bit of knowledge may be useful on the job. A good reporter reads newspapers and magazines, watches television, and listens to radio news. In effect, he becomes a news junkie.

Few television news organizations have invested in a "morgue"—that is, filed library clippings from the newspapers. When a story breaks, the reporter is expected to have in his head sufficient background to make sense out of what is happening. A good reporter can bring to almost any circumstance a background of understanding and knowledge that can help to illuminate the event for the viewer. Obviously, he cannot be expected to be a walking encyclopedia, but he ought to know enough to recognize the central issues and the chief protagonists, and he ought to know enough to ask the right questions.

In recent years, larger television stations have been moving toward wider use of specialist reporters, individuals who cover beats or specific areas of knowledge. These reporters can be expected to know more about their specialties, but they, too, need to be generally informed because so much information is interconnected.

For example, the medical and science reporter has to keep up with the politics that can shape regulations and laws affecting his area. The city hall reporter has to keep himself informed on developments on the state and federal fronts since so much of what cities can and cannot do is determined in state capitals and in Washington. Furthermore, both of these specialists have to be aware of foreign developments which can both directly and indirectly shape the news in science or in politics. Thus the specialist has to be as much a generalist as he is a specialist, and that places on him a heavy and sobering responsibility.

The reporter's capacity to challenge what people tell him will depend on his basic knowledge and his critical sense. The poorly informed reporter is likely to operate as a stenographer, reporting uncritically whatever he is told. And that is marshmallow journalism, a mindless exercise. The public has the right to expect the journalist to apply professional evaluations and judgment to the information that is gathered. The reporter who keeps informed, who evaluates news as he receives it, who can see patterns in disparate developments and make the connection, who challenges what he hears and sees, is the one who adds to the sum total of the viewer's knowledge. He imposes his intelligence on the material that is available to him.

In television reporting, it is difficult to inject that intelligence and knowledge after the fact. The reporter must bring it along with him and apply it on the scene.

CHAPTER TWO.

What Is News?

Ask any reporter what the social value of his work is, and he is likely to reply that the public has the right to know, and the reporter is the man or woman who has the duty to tell. Journalists presume that there is a public interest at stake in the free flow of information, and that explains why the Founding Fathers included freedom of the press in the First Amendment to the Constitution.

When reporters and editors decide what is news, they are in effect defining what it is in the public interest to know. In his book *The Public Philosophy* Walter Lippmann wrote that "the public interest may be presumed to be what men would choose if they saw clearly, thought rationally, acted disinterestedly and benevolently."

On occasion, the journalist's definition of news meshes neatly with Lippmann's high-minded description of the public interest. For example, seeing clearly and thinking rationally, it is plain that the public needs to understand what the government is doing, or else government secrecy could endanger the democratic system. But does it also serve the public interest to report that two movie stars have squabbled and are suing for divorce? Is it news when ten youngsters hold a frisbee contest in a midtown park? Is it in the public interest to be reminded that fires and murders, robberies and rapes took place today? Where does the highminded public interest end and the use of news as entertainment and titivation begin?

Deciding what is news is hardly an exact science. When individual journalists talk about the public interest, each has in mind a different public and a different interest. Perception of "the public" will be based in part on the audience the reporter is trying to reach and, even more, the audience that the news organization's advertisers are trying to reach. In short, what the public has the right to know, according to individual news organizations, is whatever the organization deems the public wants and needs to know. Plainly these are subjective judgments, dependent on the vision and values of those in positions of power.

Yet the process is less serendipitous or arbitrary than these comments would suggest. Like any profession, journalism has its own mindset and its particular worldview, and these are naturally and inevitably reflected in the final news product.

Perhaps nowhere is that worldview more clearly defined than in what a news organization decides is significant. News professionals argue that certain stories are obviously important: the passage of major legislation; a Presidential speech; a tornado that kills numbers of citizens. Yet even in these cases there are refinements of the larger values. Is everything that the President says equally significant? How do you define a piece of legislation as major rather than minor? And why is a tornado that kills five people more newsworthy than a car accident that kills the same number?

There are no hard and fast definitions of news, only traditions and changing demands of the consumer market. However there do exist a few general principles that newspeople apply when they are evaluating a story.

For example, news is expected to be timely and fresh. What happens today has priority over a continuing story or something that happened ten days ago. Furthermore, if it is unexpected, startling, and remarkable, then it is probably news. Airplanes fly every day and fly safely without news organizations reporting the fact. But when a plane crashes, it becomes news. It happened today. It is unexpected. It is out-of-the ordinary. In addition, it is a tragedy and tragedy is part of the stuff of news.

A local accident is of more interest than one that happens in India, just as a local flood is of more interest than one that happens a thousand miles away. The principle applied in this instance is proximity. That is, people are presumed to be more interested in an event that occurs close at hand than they are in an event that is distant and affects "outsiders." Philosophically, it can be argued that it ought not to be this way. We say that all human life has equal value, regardless of where people live or what their national origin. However, news professionals perceive that, in fact, human beings tend to care most for kin, countrymen, and neighbors, and thus a nearby or local story becomes more newsworthy than a distant one.

An event also becomes news when it involves large numbers of people, or heavy damage to property. A hurricane that destroys a hundred houses is more newsworthy than one that affects only one residence.

What the President of the United States does or says can influence the fate of the entire nation, and that makes him the biggest newsmaker of all. One might quibble that every personal item about the President—like what he eats for breakfast and the tie he wears for a social event—is hardly worth reporting, but in this case news organizations are feeding public curiosity about the man, not his job. Like other public figures, including rock stars, the President is considered fair game for features and other soft news stories of human interest.

Crime and fire stories are still big news on many local television stations, at a time when respected newspapers are tending to give these events less space. Both kinds of story fall into the "cheap-and-nasty" category of news. They are obvious, titillating, and require little in the way of intellectual effort on the part of reporters or producers of news programs. Plainly they are attractive to some television people because they involve sensational visual material—bullet holes in a door, bleeding bodies, blazing rooftops, funerals of policemen.

The best way for the neophyte reporter to recognize what is news is to read a variety of newspapers, watch television, and listen to radio. It is also a good idea for him to evaluate critically what he reads, hears, and watches.

While news is whatever a news organization says it is, there is a presumption that the people who work in the business are applying professional judgments to their labors. At times those judgments will be shaped by the demand for higher ratings and a felt need to entertain as well as inform. In time, the reporter who wants to survive learns to recognize the prevailing view of what is likely to be published or aired.

However, the new reporter who is too closely wedded to the safe, prevailing view of news can turn himself into a dull hack. The fact is, almost any trained reporter can cover set pieces like a news conference or a speech in creditable fashion. The one that makes his mark is the one who is capable of originating fresh ideas, the kind of reporter who refuses to follow the pack but instead proposes his own stories and issues to be covered.

The best of news stories spring from the intelligence, imagination, and curiosity of a thinking individual. One of the characteristics that separates one news organization from another is the enterprise story, born out of the head of a creative reporter or producer. The eager and ambitious young journalist can build a strong reputation inside his organization if he regularly comes up with fresh angles and original reports.

It is likely that much of what could be news today is not news simply because nobody is reporting it. In the decades before the sixties, the news media virtually ignored the rumblings of the imminent black revolution because few reporters (there were very few black reporters then—and not many more now—who might have been more sensitive to what was happening) cared to look, see, and notice. How many other stories lie hidden and untold today, it is impossible to judge. But you can be sure that they are there, and the reporter who has his antennae up and his blinders off can find them if he wants to.

Where do story ideas come from? First, quite simply, from the reporter's direct observations and life experiences. A good reporter hardly ever stops working. If a neighbor injures himself by walking blindly into and then shattering a plate glass door, the reporter thinks: "why are these doors made this way, without somebody considering the possible dangers?" He has the beginnings of a story. He buys a new house and discovers it is poorly finished and filled with flaws. He talks with his neighbors and he finds that they have been having similar problems. Is this a common experience among new homeowners? What protections do consumers have against builders who put up shoddy new homes? Wherever the reporter finds himself—at a school board meeting, a bus stop, a dinner party—he is listening to the problems, worries, and concerns of the people around him.

The key to generating stories is a combination of awareness, sensitivity, the capacity to ask the right questions, and the willingness to ask "dumb" ones. One of the most useful of questions is "why?"

The best reporters are haunted by a strong sense of how things ought to be, or might be. Many of the most significant news stories grow out of the difference between how things are and how they should be.

Examine for a moment the hoopla that follows the passage of major legislation. The law is passed and the politicians have announced what they intend for it. These are reportable facts, but down the road apiece some enterprising reporter could make news by finding out if, in fact, the law is doing what it was supposed to do. Is it just keeping bureaucrats busy, wasting taxpayer money, forcing recipients to fill out extra forms? If the law is not doing what was intended for it, is it fixable? And why did it go wrong?

Too few reporters take the time and trouble to pursue a story once it is no longer in the public eye. This often leaves the impression with the reader and viewer that a certain social problem has been solved by the simple passage of a law. In order to do his job properly, the reporter who covered the original story needs to keep close to the circumstances that follow implementation of the law. In this way the reporter fulfills the watchdog role of the media, a job as important to the public as the reporting of the legislative and executive actions of officials.

How do you accomplish this? You carefully develop contacts during the deliberations on the bill and at the time that it is signed into law. It is then that public officials are most available and likely to be delighted by your interest in the subject. After the bill becomes law, you phone your contacts at regular intervals just to see how things are progressing. Contact the groups of citizens who are supposed to be helped by the legislation, and let them know that you care about them and how the legislation affects them.

Take the time to visit the site of the action. Scrutinize the quality and character of the staff that is hired. Keep in touch. Show both officials and citizens that you are concerned, even though the story is no longer a major event. In the end, they are likely to phone you not just about this particular story but about any others that come their way.

In effect, what you do is build up a network of eyes and ears that keep you in touch with experiences and realities other than your own. Compound this network with other networks that you have developed while covering other events, and you have developed a useful way of keeping in touch with what is happening well beyond the limits of your own life and experience.

The all too easy way to cover news is to wait for some official to call a news conference or to stage an event. Unfortunately, some television news organizations jump too quickly to the snap of these fingers. The result often is that the news source manipulates the news. His chief purpose is to sell his story on his own terms and in his own time, and he often succeeds.

Due attention has to be given to official news, but a good reporter will not be satisfied with that. Even where the story grows out of a planned event, he will look for something more, some way to make the human, citizen connection.

For example, Mayor X calls a news conference to announce that he has assigned more police officers to Precinct Y, and as a result crime is down in that area. Is what the Mayor says true, or just a piece of public relations? You will, of course, allow the Mayor to have his say, but don't be satisfied with this single component of your story. Afterwards, visit Precinct Y and talk with the local police and residents. Also try to ascertain which other precinct is now short of police manpower because of the Mayor's decision to reassign personnel. In sum, the big political pronouncement at city hall can look remarkably different down at the grass roots, where the real action is.

Remember that news is about people. There are fine, powerful stories about citizens on the front lines of change. A new zoning law is passed. How will it affect the people who live in or near that area? A neighborhood is declining. Who is left behind, and how do these residents feel about the changes and how are they coping? Inflation mounts: how do people manage their finances, what do they do without, how do they perceive the chances for a better life in the future? The human dimensions of social, economic, and political upheavals are always news and newsworthy.

It is important to particularize as well as to give the grand abstraction. Television offers a marvelous opportunity to expose the texture of lives that are individual as well as part of a group. Television news can humanize an issue or a problem by giving it a face, a voice, a living reality—by offering up the curious uniqueness of this particular person in place of the graphs, the charts, and the social scientist's groupings.

Of course the reporter must be careful not to leave the impression that all of the group is like the particular member of the group who is being interviewed; but it is useful to put a human face on a social problem.

There is a growing conviction that the only truth that can be verified and therefore that is worth reporting is one that can be measured, weighed, and catalogued in precise mathematical terms. Yet to the average citizen numbers and charts lack a certain something, a dimension that is incalculable and yet very real.

"Independent voters feel this way," say the pollsters. But who are these independent voters? What makes them tick? Why do they choose to keep themselves unaligned? The polls, the charts, and the mathematical calculations are useful in tracing the larger picture—but the *human meaning* of it is lost without the connection to flesh-and-blood people. Television news, handled with care and discipline, can make this connection and, in the process, add an important dimension to public caring and understanding of larger issues.

Learn to listen with your mind and your heart. Sometimes you are doing a story on one subject, and another potential story crops up. Make a mental note of it, and follow up at a later time.

Read. Read everything you can lay your hands on, and read actively instead of passively. Mull over the material and ideas. Frame spin-off questions. For example, you read that unemployment among black teenagers is persistently high and going up. You ask yourself why is this so? Who are these young people? What jobs are available? What skills do they have? What training programs are offered? What is the nature of their hopes, dreams, visions of their society? The key question again is *why?* and in the search for answers there are a thousand stories waiting to be told. Journalism is at its best when it explains what is hidden under the surface and what lies ahead.

Expand your horizons. To view the world only from your safe, private, middle-class point of view is to limit the scope of your reporting. Enterprise news is news at the edge of shift and change. You should be out front, your nose in the air, sniffing for new moods, changing loyalties, fresh perceptions. To succeed you will need to develop the habit of talking with all kinds of people, particularly people who lead lives different from your own. Avoid becoming the kind of reporter who is always following the crowd and the latest "in" story.

Once you have been reporting for awhile, you will develop a collection of contacts—people to whom you can turn for ideas and leads. Develop the habit of phoning these people on a regular basis to ask them how they are and what is happening in their lives and communities. By showing that you care about them and their constituencies you will be building the kind of relationship that will give you, the lone reporter, the chance to effectively reshape your organization's definition of news.

Be skeptical. You will read some remarkably silly statements in your morning paper. Sometimes a good story can be made out of exposing a statement as wrong or downright malicious. Try not to be dazzled by budgets and statistics. Make your own independent analysis of the figures that you obtain. Find out how the official arrived at the figures. Seek out an analysis from assorted nonofficial experts. It is not your job to accept blindly and then to report blandly whatever sources tell you, but rather to apply a hard-nosed "show-me" approach to whatever you read, see, and hear.

Care. Care a lot. Passion and fire-in-the-belly may not be fashionable, but they are powerful assets in the best reporters. They must be controlled, of course. That is, they should not be allowed to cloud judgment or cover up unpalatable information. But this quality of caring about a story can help you to stay with it even when the leads seem to be going nowhere. When you care about the people who are making the news or are affected by it, the reporting and the writing improve visibly.

There is as great a need for enterprise reporting in print journalism as there is in broadcasting. However, the television reporter has an additional consideration when he is trying to sell his story idea to the news desk. Whether he will be granted time and facilities to pursue a story can depend not only on the story's intrinsic value, but on how he plans to translate the idea into something visual.

In short, in television news, it is not enough to have a good idea. It has to be a good *television* idea, and that means the reporter must think of ways to turn the story into pictures. If all you have in mind is a "talking head," a rather dry interview with somebody simply talking into the camera, you may have difficulty obtaining a camera crew to be assigned to your story. On the other hand, if you can project an interesting setting, or a lively bit of action, and if you have a proven gift for eliciting the dramatic heart of a story from your interviews, permission may be granted.

Do not expect to win all of your struggles with the news desk. Some assignment editors prefer stock stories because they can be sure that a camera crew assigned to a ten o'clock news conference will be free to cover something else at eleven. By contrast, the enterprise story is uncertain in shape and the commitment of time and cameras has to be virtually open-ended.

Remember that, while you are arguing the case for your enterprise story, the assignment editor has to fit your proposal into his estimate of the availability of facilities that day, as well as the producer's overall plans for the news program. The editor may prefer to play it safe rather than gamble on a story that is not listed in the daybook.

Many a noble and promising television news story has gone untold for want of logistical support. This, sadly, is a fact of life, and one of the more common frustrations faced by reporters who want to be enterprising and creative.

CHAPTER THREE.

Mastering the Technology and Reporting in the Field, Part 1

The tools of the trade for a print reporter working in the field are a pencil (or a ballpoint pen) and a notepad. Some print reporters also use a tape recorder to make sure that the quotes they obtain are exact quotes.

By comparison with the tools of a television reporter, these are simplicity itself. Reporters who move from careers in print to careers in television find themselves in a strange new world where the demands of the technology often seem to get in the way of the story. So terrifying is the experience that some new reporters experience nightmares in which they find themselves tangled up in cords and cables, or doomed to oblivion by malfunctioning lights, failed cameras, and mysterious disappearances in editing rooms.

The television reporter has to learn to live with the fact that his technology is imperfect; that as it grows more refined and complex, it requires skilled technicians to control it and to fix it, and that often the machines simply break down or the human beings goof. The reporter needs to learn to overcome "technical difficulties" with humor, skill, and ingenuity, to get the story to the people in spite of unexpected technological obstacles.

The key word is *control*. Remember that your mission is to get the story and to tell it well. Therefore you have to control the technology so that it serves those purposes and not itself.

A vital difference between print reporting and electronic reporting is that basically the print reporter works alone, while the television reporter interacts with his camera crew in the field and with the production staff at the station. TV news is a team effort.

In the field you will be working with one, two, or three people, depending on the union agreement operating within the news organization. Normally your crew will consist of a camera operator and a technician. In smaller and medium-sized markets, the crew for a videotape story is often one person. However many there are in your crew, you should understand clearly what their responsibilities are, and how you interact with them.

The camera operator is responsible for shooting the scenes necessary to make up the final package. He also puts up tripods and lights, where necessary, and connects the required cables and cords. The technician helps him to put up the lights and does related chores. The technician's chief job is to operate the videocassette recorder (VCR), which captures the pictures and sound as they are filmed by the camera. It is his job to ensure the quality of the sound in interviews, stand-ups, narration recorded in the field, and natural sound, as well as to operate the microwave gear.

On most occasions, the reporter is also the field producer. This means that, in addition to the responsibility for covering the story, writing news copy, and delivering it, he is responsible for the content of the visual material that will later be edited into a news story. In other words, out in the field, the reporter is in command of the team. It is he who determines where the camera team should go, what it should shoot, and even when the videotape is to be shipped back to the newsroom. These are executive skills, and a television news reporter must exercise those skills with the same diligence, responsibility, and tact that any other kind of executive must employ.

It is extremely important for the reporter to understand the demands of the technology and the technicians, and to understand both their human and mechanical limitations. Unfortunately, union rules in most news organizations preclude a reporter from working the camera or physically editing his own material. At the Columbia University Graduate School of Journalism, all students who take the news reporting course in television are required to take turns operating the cameras and editing the videotape. By having to deal with both the onerousness and the beauty of the medium, the students come away with more respect for, and understanding of, the technical side of the business. However, even where this direct grounding in the technology is unavailable, the reporter can learn a great deal by asking questions of the camera crew.

To repeat, it is essential that the reporter understand the mechanics of shooting and the technical requirements for shaping a news package. However, even as he masters these techniques, he must keep in the forefront of his mind the essential thrust and character of the story itself.

Most news stories begin the way that a scientist begins his experiment— with an idea or a theory. It is fruitless to launch an experiment without a sense of purpose, and it is the same with news reporting. As soon as the reporter has his assignment in hand, he must begin to theorize about it. What is its significance? Who are the chief actors? What are the issues? What is likely to happen?

A typical assignment would be this one: The Mayor has called a news conference at City Hall to talk about crime. The kinds of questions you should ask yourself are these:

• Why is the Mayor calling a news conference at this time? What recent events have occurred that might have impelled him to do so?

• Have there been recent conflicts between the Mayor and the city's police chief? What is the substance of those conflicts?

• What are the central issues in the city's crime controversy? Too few police on the streets? Inept prosecutors? Lax courts? Increasing poverty and unemployment? Guns?

• What is the political background to all of this? Is the Mayor running for reelection? Who is he running against? How is this situation likely to affect the Mayor's statements on crime?

• What is the true nature of the crime problem, and is it within the power of any mayor to solve it? If not, who can? How?

After this period of rumination on the event you are about to cover, move on to practical considerations: how to get to the news conference; how much time is available to do the story and to meet the deadline; how best to use the resources of time, camera, and reporter.

If there is sufficient time available before the event, do some research and make some informational phone calls. Don't go out stumbling and groping for an idea. One of the most serious failures of beginning television news reporters is the failure to *focus*, and to focus early.

This preplanning or theorizing ought not to be so inflexible that you are unable to change direction on arrival, should the story subsequently turn out to be different. But to attempt to "play it by ear" right from the start, is to open the way for vague, imprecise, and shallow reporting. Remember that television does not lend itself to broad overview stories. It is better to do a narrow story, precisely focused, and from there to generalize somewhat.

From the beginning, involve the camera crew in all aspects of the story. Tell the cameraperson in particular that you are looking for a specific statement, a certain angle, and solicit the help of the camera to capture both the mood and the substance of this material. Often, a cameraperson has good news judgment, and can offer useful advice and suggestions.

On this point, Kenneth Tiven, the news director at station WPXI in Pittsburgh, adds these comments: "Young reporters can be very much like young lawyers. They have an excellent grasp of the theory of journalism, but precious little sense of the daily details of newsgathering.

"Veteran cameracrews can be invaluable in explaining how to gather information, and how to find and collect the interviews that are vital.

"Furthermore, camera crews are sensitive to how intrusive the equipment can be in a given situation, and their reaction to a series of events, while not always accurate, can serve as an interesting and valuable barometer."

When you are in the field, it is wise to give the cameraperson "loose rein" to shoot extra footage that would be useful in the story. An intelligent and creative photojournalist can add immeasurably to any story by capturing pictorial vignettes or eloquent visuals that make a story more interesting, relevant, and eyecatching. He will also see many things that you may miss while you are busy setting up interviews, writing a script or a stand-up, or simply covering a breaking story.

The wise reporter learns early how to employ and harness the valuable talents of his news team, to bring out the best in the members of that team, so that the final news product is an amalgam of many talents stretched to their utmost. In addition, it is important for the reporter to give praise where praise is due. In television news it is the reporter who is out front, in the starring role. Yet the end product is the result of efforts by many people. The reporter who recognizes and appreciates fine technical work, shooting, sound, and editing, would be wise to share his feelings with his colleagues. Anyone will do better work if he knows it is valued and appreciated.

Furthermore, the reporter who behaves like a prima donna is less likely to produce an outstanding story than the one who learns to work amicably and creatively with the camera crew and editor. It is all very well for a reporter to have an idea for his story, but without the active cooperation of the technicians, it can come to nothing.

Now to consider some basic principles for the use of the television camera in the reporting process.

RULE ONE   Do not use the camera as a pad and pencil

For the name of the person being interviewed, his background, occupation, address, for basic background information of any kind, do what the print reporter does—write it down. However, it is also wise to have the person interviewed identify himself on camera at the beginning of the interview. This will help to avoid later confusion if you are doing a number of interviews. Furthermore, be sure that you have in your notebook the correct spelling of the individual's name as well as the correct title.

While you are in the field you should be thinking of the final shape of the story. You will find that you are not likely to want to use a piece of videotape in which the news source is stating his name, address, and occupation, so only shoot the name for identification purposes.

You will also find that it is better to return to the newsroom with less videotape instead of more, because under the pressure of deadlines, the editor prefers not to have to wind through useless footage.

RULE TWO   Use the camera with economy

Use it with *purpose* and economy. There is nothing more wasteful than scattershot shooting—aiming at this and that, without any idea of what it all adds up to. To shoot a nice picture that is totally irrelevant to the story at hand shows a lack of discipline and direction. It is also exasperating for the editor who has to view the results of your work.

Rules one and two indicate some of the restraints on the use of the camera. What then do you use the camera for? Use it for what the camera does best: illuminate facts, reveal emotion, set a scene, humanize abstractions.

If you are covering a speech or a news conference, or if you are doing an interview, remember that you are aiming to use only a small piece of this effort on the air. Perhaps fifteen seconds (or, where the story warrants it, it might be ninety seconds) of a statement or reply will actually make it to air. If you regularly watch television news programs, both local and network, you will see how brief the "sound-bites" are. A sound-bite is that part of the news story in which somebody (other than the reporter) is speaking in his own words on camera. It is quite surprising how much can be said and the impact of those few words, if they are chosen judiciously. Your job, then, is to decide which revealing nugget you need to tell your story.

For example: The Mayor calls a news conference to announce the resignation of the deputy mayor and the appointment of a new deputy. Do you intend to use the footage of the announcement itself, or isn't the fact of the resignation and appointment likely to be the lead of the story, delivered by the anchorperson in the studio? Having reported on camera that Mr. Z. resigned, and Ms. O will take his place, the anchorperson will then lead to the reporter, who will tell . . . what? The same thing?

No. If in the field you are thinking of the final news package, you will realize that the body of the reporter's story will contain not the lead, the headline, the hard facts, but *the reasons why.* In short, what you are looking for *on videotape* is not the announcement itself, but the followup explanation and the challenges to the explanation in the question-and-answer part of the news conference.

The same principle applies in an interview. If Councilman Q. says he opposes the actions of Councilman R., that is probably going to be the lead of the story. What you want *on videotape* from Councilman Q. is his argument in favor of his position and in opposition to the position of Councilman R. Knowing that, in your interview, you aim your questions for that particular kernel or essence of the story. Of course you may not get a satisfactory explanation the first time that you ask the questions. You may have to parry, challenge, even counter the Councilman's arguments with those put forward by his opponent. But all the time, you know in your head what it is that you are looking for in the way of a sound-bite, and you use the camera to fulfill that purpose.

The skilled TV reporter is always operating on at least two levels: he is interviewing or listening for information, but at the same time, he is packaging the final news story in his head. When he finds the sound-bite he needs and wants, and when it comes in a shape he believes to be lively and editable, a little bell goes off in his head—a tiny "aha!"—and he then asks the cameraperson to turn off the camera.

Remember that in telling your story you are not limited to using the sound-bite alone. That is merely one element, although an important one, in the final package. You also have the option to use pictures that you will talk over. These are called "voice-overs."

If you intend to write a voice-over, then you should make sure that, after you have your sound-bite safely in hand, the cameraperson shoots the kinds of pictures that can be used to illustrate and back up your script. Again, you can see that you are making vital judgments in the field. As a television reporter you do not have the luxury of returning to the newsroom to mull over what the story should be before you write it and package it. If you come back without pictures that fit your script, you are in hot water with the editor. You may even be forced to reshape the entire story to fit what is available as a visual.

Fortunately, there are a number of standard, general cover shots that your cameraperson will normally shoot during a story. For example, at a news conference, he will give you a wide shot that sets the scene, a picture of the speaker listening to the questions, a picture of reporters taking notes and of cameras rolling. This general material is the kind of videotape that is serviceable for voice-overs, although it is hardly exciting visually. But don't take it for granted that the camera operator has these shots on videotape. Make sure that the cameraperson has taken them before the crew breaks away from the scene. Remember that it is your responsibility to bring back what is necessary to edit a story successfully, even though the person running the camera does the actual shooting.

So far we have touched on three potential elements in the total television news story:

The anchor lead-in: The lead, or headline of the story, as drafted by the reporter for a producer, and read by the anchorperson. The lead-in carries the story to the reporter. Example:

ANCHOR OC (on camera): Mayor X today announced the resignation of Deputy Mayor Z and the appointment of a local lawyer, O, to take his place. Robyn Smith has more on the story.

The voice-over: The reporter, speaking over a series of edited pictures, telling additional elements of the story, and leading up to the sound bite. Example:

SMITH VO/VTR (voice over videotape): The Mayor says the mounting friction between himself and his deputy makes it impossible for them to continue as a team. He says it's important to the city for both to share the same goals. He lists these areas of disagreement that led to Z.'s resignation.

Sound-Bite: This is videotape of the news source, in this case the Mayor himself. Example:

MAYOR SOT (sound on tape): "Z. failed to support my efforts to change the zoning laws. He tried to block my plans to cut the number of police and sanitationmen. He resisted the fare increase for the buses. In short, he made it impossible for me to govern this city."

The above is not yet a complete story; but it illustrates some of the elements you must make sure that you have in hand:

1. A *lead* for the anchorperson which gives the story its central theme and focus.

2. Sufficient *visuals* to cover your voice-over script at the beginning of the story.

3. A *sound-bite* that goes to the heart of the story, without repeating information that is in the anchor lead-in and the voice-over.

In sum, even as the story unfolds, you must be mapping out the shape of the final product, and thinking ahead to what more is needed in both journalistic and visual terms.

Earlier in this chapter, reference was made to the need for executive leadership by the television news reporter. One of the most important ways that leadership is exercised is in the efficient use of the camera team's time. In most news organizations, the reporter has the use of the camera crew for a limited time—perhaps an hour or two—since the crew is likely to be assigned elsewhere later. Knowing that, the pressure is on the reporter to make swift judgments about the news story so that all the visual elements are in place before the crew is reassigned. Sometimes even the reporter is reassigned to cover something else. At small TV stations, it is not unknown for a reporter to produce three and four stories each day.

Even while he has the crew, the reporter must be aware of other deadlines: the time it takes to travel, to ship the videotape back to the station, to edit, to write and record the voice-over. The final deadline is of course *air time* for the news program.

Not many years ago, most television stations ran their news operations with film instead of videotape. The use of film slowed the delivery of the news product considerably, since film has to be processed in a chemical bath before it can be viewed and edited. By contrast, videotape is ready to be edited the moment that it is shot. When the live minicams (portable electronic cameras) are connected to a van on which a microwave sending dish is mounted, the microwave signals can be beamed directly back to the station, where the signals are translated into pictures. The videotape can thus be viewed in the newsroom even as it is shot, and editing can begin immediately. However, this procedure is normally used only for major, breaking stories. Usually the videotape has to be physically returned to the newsroom from the field.

Like any other executive, the TV reporter has to be aware of union rules in regard to the members of the camera crew, and plan his shooting around them. Some stations do not allow the reporter to cancel a coffee or lunch break, which would entail paying overtime. The reporter must therefore accommodate his shooting schedule to that reality, too. Where the reporter has doubts about the rules, and what he can and cannot do in the way of overseeing the camera crew, he should call the news desk at the station for clarification. While the reporter is in charge in the field, he still has to take his direction from the assignment editor, executive producer, or news director back at the station.

From all of this you can gather that the work of the television news reporter is different from that of the newspaper or magazine reporter. While he shares the same responsibility for fairness, accuracy, balance, and depth, he must also worry about the technological and economic demands of the medium. It is not enough for him to obtain the information necessary to shape a news story. He has to get it in a form that is visual or that can be translated into something visual. His labor requires a melding of instant news judgment, creative imagination, executive skill, precision writing, and the kind of stamina and calm that allows him to go on camera looking cool and self-possessed.

Plainly, this is not a profession that suits all temperaments.

CHAPTER FOUR.

Mastering the Technology and Reporting In the Field, Part 2

Television requires the reporter to do a modicum of acting. As does the actor, the reporter has to be aware of where he sits, how he moves, and what the camera demands. Some reporters find this aspect of their work to be a nuisance. They would prefer instead to focus their energies on the content of the story. However, there is no escaping the performance requirements of the television news business. The sooner that the reporter masters the basic "stage" principles, the sooner can he perform these movements automatically, and thereby leave himself time and energy to concentrate on journalism.

The hard fact is that an awkwardly constructed picture can detract from a good and solid story. Certain movements are required of the reporter simply because these result in the kinds of pictures that can be properly edited later on. A dedicated cameraperson will help you to sit or stand correctly, but not all of those who run cameras will care enough to help you to learn the necessary stagecraft.

Begin with the interview: where do you stand when you are talking to a news source? To answer that question, it is best to consider what picture you think the camera should see. Beginning reporters tend to think that their faces and bodies should be seen in every shot. As a result, the untutored reporter is likely to try the "crab" shot. He will sit at the side of the person interviewed and face directly into the camera. He will thus be forced to twist his body sideways in order to position the microphone. As a result, the only thing the camera sees of the interviewee is a profile. Plainly, this kind of picture makes no sense. What in fact the camera (and through the camera's eye, the television viewer) wants to see, *needs* to see during the interview, is the full face of the person being interviewed and if possible none of the reporter at all.

The reason for this is simple: It is more effective to see the interviewee's face and to hear him talk as if he were captured in a natural setting rather than in a formalized interview. Furthermore, for editing purposes, it is easier to cut from one shot of the interviewee to another shot without having to try to match up the movements of another figure on the screen.

The best way to obtain the proper picture is to stand in front of, but slightly to the side of, the subject, with your *back* to the camera. The microphone should be held low, about mid-chest, so that it does not cover the news source's face; if the cameraperson shoots the picture right, the microphone will not be seen at all. Since these microphones are very sensitive, there is no need to press one up against the face of the subject. *Neither do you have to move the microphone back and forth between yourself and the subject.*

When time permits it is helpful to use two small lavalier-type microphones instead of one hand-held microphone. This makes it easier to forget the presence of the microphones and it helps to relax the news source. It also frees the reporter's hands for note-taking, and creates a more natural-looking picture.

For the person running the camera, the picture should show the news subject in close-up or a medium close-up, looking slightly to the side and front to answer your questions. There should be no sign of your shoulder, and if you have a habit of swaying into the picture, the camera should be stopped, and you should be instructed to stand still.

Before the camera begins to roll, the cameraperson should set up the shot. If he is unhappy with the way you and the subject are standing, he should walk over and gently position both of you. Don't begin the interview until you have the signal from the cameraperson. (The usual signal is the word "rolling.") The videotape should always roll at least seven seconds before the signal is given, and the camera should always roll at least ten seconds beyond the interview at the end. All of these details help in the later editing of the videotape.

Signal to the cameraperson that the interview is over by saying to the news source, "thank you very much." Then stand still while the camera operator runs off some extra footage, again for editing purposes.

Suppose that you are in a news source's house and you want to interview him while he is sitting on his sofa. Try to do the interview with both of you sitting at the same level. If you fail to do this, the news source will be looking *up* at you to answer questions, or looking *down*. The resulting picture caught by the camera will appear both unnatural and awkward. You might use a small straight chair and sit in front of, but slightly to the side of, the news subject. Or, you could sit face to face on the sofa. In order to avoid the crab shot, the cameraperson would shoot over one arm of the sofa, but still over the reporter's shoulder as well. The point is to try to shoot the story in such a way that it can be edited without much difficulty, regardless of the setting in which the interview takes place.

The interview is the bread-and-butter of television news. You will find yourself doing interviews in all kinds of places—on street corners, at the edge of burning wreckage, in the cramped quarters of a slum apartment. You are going to have to learn to adapt the visual techniques to the particular situation, working very closely with the man or woman behind the camera. Sometimes it will be necessary for you to be shown during the interview. Some local stations even prefer that their reporters be in evidence, because they see their reporters as personalities who should be highly visible. You should adapt your style to the news organization for which you are working.

There will be times when a fast-breaking news story will require that you move in quickly with your microphone without time to set up the camera shot. In such circumstances you have to leave it to the cameraperson to capture the scene as best he can. However, even then it helps if you can remain aware of the camera's requirements and try to avoid blocking the picture or making it hard for the photographer to do his job.

When arranging the setting for an interview, be aware of several technical considerations. The wrong background can create problems with lighting, or it can provide a distraction during the interview. The electronic camera is a highly adaptable instrument. It contains a filter which can be adjusted to different lighting circumstances. However, when the source of the lighting is mixed—that is, in a situation where natural light from a window combines with fluorescent light in an office, the camera filter that is adjusted for one light source is inappropriate to the other, and the result is a poor color picture. The camera operator should decide which of the two available light sources he will use during the interview.

Similar difficulties can arise where there is glare. Plain white walls can distort and reflect light, while a background of heavy drapes, which absorb too much light, leaves the interview subject sitting in front of what appears to be a dark cave. You should understand why your cameraperson is fussing over these details and patiently cooperate until the correct lighting is arranged.

In addition to showing concern for the lighting of an interview, the reporter and technicians must consider the background. A busy office with jangling telephones and workers moving back and forth may provide a semblance of cinéma vérité, but at the same time distract from the interview itself. A streetcorner interview or stand-up can introduce the vital bustle of the city, but it also brings the noise of the city's buses, trucks, and sirens into the microphone. Furthermore, the camera tends to attract curious onlookers, especially street kids, who will stand behind you, mugging and joking, during your stand-up.

The reporter and his technical crew must weigh these considerations and balance the search for realism against the potential for visual and aural distraction in a particular setting.

The camera has a zoom lens which should be used with great care. Constant zooming in and out during an interview makes it hard for the editor later on and anyhow, it is always best to keep things simple. However, if a speaker or an interviewee grows angry, emotional, or agitated, the camera should zoom in carefully to reveal the face in a tight close-up. The viewer will want to see the glitter of the eyes, the sweat on the brow, the twitch in the jaw, and an alert cameraperson will capture these visible signs of emotion. Also at some point, but not in the middle of a statement, the cameraperson might want to change the shot from a medium close-up to a wide shot or a close-up. This will offer some variety for the editor to work with later. But again, the cameraperson should not overdo it; camera work should be controlled and purposeful, not dizzying.

You have just completed your interview, but your work is not yet over. Suppose the interview has to be edited? Suppose that you want to take a piece of an answer here and butt it up against a piece of an answer later on? How are you going to get the picture to move from one place to the other?

If you simply edit the two sound-bites together, you will have what is called a "jump cut" at the point of edit: the head, the mouth, the movements will be in a different position on either side of the edit, and the result will be an odd, jerky, and distracting picture. To avoid a jump cut, you have to shoot a picture called a *cutaway*. What the cutaway does is cover over the cut with another picture, so that you hear the sound, but for a brief time you see something other than the person who is speaking. For editing purposes this is a vital shot, not only to cover a jump cut, but sometimes it is used to break the visual monotony of a long statement by changing to another picture. Some networks, especially CBS, have recently taken the position that the edits should be seen and not covered by cutaways, on the ground that this is more honest. While it is true that videotape jump cuts are not so distracting as film cuts, the cutaway practice remains the norm.

In the interview situation, the most obvious cutaway is a picture of the reporter listening to the person who is speaking. But since you have only one camera, and that camera has been shooting the face of the person interviewed, how can it also capture a picture of the face of the listening reporter?

Simple. After the interview is over, the camera is moved around to the other side. It shoots a picture of you, standing where you were before, and making believe that you are listening to the interviewee. This is another piece of acting, but quite necessary to the editing process. Hold the microphone as you did during the interview and look both lively and intelligent while the camera rolls. Avoid moving your head up and down as though you were agreeing with what you have heard. Reporters are not supposed to agree or disagree, just get the facts. Besides, an editor might inadvertently edit in a reporter's approving nod just when the news subject is saying something outrageous. (This has been known to happen in the most professional of organizations.) To avoid the possibility of this happening to you, "listen" quietly and attentively, but without nodding, when you do your cutaways.

Now comes a more complicated piece of stagecraft. If, as seen in the camera, the subject's head is pointing to the *right*, the cutaway shot of you as you listen should be pointing the *opposite* way. Otherwise, when the two pieces of tape are edited, it will look like the two participants were looking *away from*, instead of *at* each other.

The rule here is just the opposite of the Biblical admonition to "turn the other cheek." When doing cutaways, you want to be sure that the cameraperson is shooting the reporter's *same cheek*. That is, if the reporter's left cheek is facing the camera for the interview, it should be the same cheek facing it for the cutaways (see figures 1 and 2).

If you can persuade the subject of the interview to stay for the cutaways, it is more effective to shoot over his shoulder at the reporter listening. But make sure that you do not see the subject's lips moving (the jaw is okay) because it is impossible to match his moving lips to what he would be saying on the sound-bites. If the subject cannot remain on the scene, the cutaways will simply be of you listening.

Returning to an earlier point—that the reporter has to organize the time of the camera crew—here is one more item that must be considered—the necessity to do cutaways. Sufficient time has to be allowed for this work, but if you and the camera crew know what you are doing and why, the procedure can be handled swiftly and efficiently.

Sometimes in a longer interview you will want to use some of the reporter's questions as well as the answers to those questions. On such occasions, it is useful to have videotape of the questions being asked; but once again, you face the problem of showing the reporter's face when the camera is focused on the person interviewed. The answer to this problem is the *reverse question.*

A reverse question is the same question that you asked during the interview, only this time you repeat it for the camera afterward. While sitting or standing in the same position that you used for the listening-shot cutaways, you reenact your part of the interview.

The reporter who plans to use reverse questions faces several problems. First, he has to remember exactly what he asked or else take notes during the interview. Some reporters tape record the interview and then play back the tape so that they can word their questions precisely as they did the first time. Or else, the reporter can run back the videotape in the camera, and using an earplug, listen to the questions through the camera.

You can clean up a question when you re-do it; that is, tighten the syntax and remove any um's and ah's. However, be careful not to change the tenor or meaning of the question, since this would give a false and unfair impression of the answer given earlier by the news source.

The next problem is to consider whether you want to use all of the questions in your interview (which is unlikely), and if not, which of them might be useful for the final editing. Having decided on the reverse questions that

What the Camera Sees

NEWS SUBJECT

REPORTER

The Reporter's left cheek is
angled toward the camera

CAMERA

Figure 1. As seen in the camera, the subject is facing to the *right*.

What the Camera Sees

REPORTER

NEWS SUBJECT

The Reporter's left cheek is still
angled toward the camera

CAMERA

Figure 2. As seen in the camera, the reporter is facing to the *left*, looking at the subject.

you want to re-do, you have to pretend that you are asking them for the first time, making your face look lively and interested even if the news subject is no longer on the scene. This requires acting of an imaginative order since in fact you will be asking questions of thin air.

Sometimes the interviewee is willing to remain on the scene while you do your reverses, in which case he may decide to answer the questions again. Remember that your chief purpose is to tape the reverse questions. However, often the subject will answer this second time with a more interesting or more concise response. Allow the interviewee to answer. You may find that you obtain a better reply this time, or one that melds nicely into the original. Remember that the videotape that you shoot can be reused, so in certain situations, where you are obtaining better material, it does no harm to shoot the answers again.

Furthermore, by incorporating in your new question necessary information from an earlier response that was too long, you can use a reverse to set up the critical answer.

For example: During a long interview with the warden at the city's main prison, you ask the following question and elicit the subsequent response:

Question: What can you do about getting health care for first offenders?

Answer: "It's a problem. I won't deny it is, because you see—um—a lot of these young fellows come to us, and you might say, they have, they have problems—TB, bad eyes, alcoholics, you name it, everything you can think of. Well, the way the jails are, you see, overcrowded, we have one-hundred percent overcrowding you know—yeah, one hundred percent—well, we can't handle this kind of thing. We don't have enough room for them, let alone the money or doctors to look after them, not even the space. We've got to persuade the city's taxpayers and the state's taxpayers to pay for what we need because it is the only fair and decent thing to do, and I personally am going to lobby hard at city hall and in the state capital to help raise money to take care of these first offenders, because if we put them in jail but we don't make them well, they'll be back again, you can count on it."

The above is a long and complicated reply, but it contains nuggets of information that you want to incorporate in your edited story. Recognizing that your airtime is limited, you will try to find a way to convey vital information without consuming too many precious seconds. A re-drafted reverse question offers you one option. Your new question would be: *If the problem of one hundred percent overcrowding in the jail continues,* what can you do about getting health care for first offenders?

The italicized portion of the reverse has been added, but in this way you can begin the warden's reply with the sound-bite that gets directly to the point: "We've got to persuade the city's taxpayers. . . . they'll be back again, you can count on it." The reverse question incorporates information just obtained in the interview. It thus makes unnecessary the use of airtime for that particular part of the response in the sound-bite.

This process differs only slightly from the rearrangements made by print reporters when they reorder the placement of direct quotes, or paraphrase in such a way as to clarify the intent and meaning of the interviewed subject. The difference is that the television reporter has to achieve the same goal, but within the limits of a brief time span and for a medium that requires the reordering and paraphrasing to be done by visual methods. This is not in fact "showbiz" as some print-schooled critics glibly charge. It is a necessary and valid way to overcome the difficulties that confront reporters who are working in a visual medium. As long as these methods do not pervert the meaning of the event, or give a false impression of the substance of the news source's reply, they are acceptable. Furthermore, they are certainly more honorable journalistically than the methods of some print reporters who reconstruct direct quotes from memory, paraphrase outrageously, draw composite pictures from a number of sources, reconstruct conversations which took place when the reporter was not present, or cite unnamed and possibly nonexistent sources.

No matter what the medium, the reporter has to be careful that the tools of his trade do not unfairly and improperly reshape the events he is reporting. But any form of journalism reshapes the event in *some* way, and there is no use pretending otherwise.

Reverse questions are most likely to be used in a long, sit-down interview. In a breaking news situation, there may be time only for cutaways. In addition, the final sound bites will probably be too short to require the interposition of a reverse question. In any case, you are acting as your own field producer, and must decide whether or not the situation warrants the taping of reverse questions. If you think so, allow sufficient crew time to get that part of the job done. The key here is to think ahead to the exigencies of the editing process. There is nothing more frustrating than to return from a story without the necessary visual shots to allow proper editing.

Listening shots are not the only possible cutaways, although they are the standard kind. A creative journalist will look for alternative pictures that may be filmed after the interview.

Are there children in the room listening (but not talking)? Are there photos or bric-a-brac that may illustrate a point or illuminate a personality? Are the subject's hands covered in rings or are the hands themselves particularly expressive and mobile? Are there objects on the scene that are relevant to material mentioned by the person being interviewed? These are all potential cutaways, and good ones, too.

For example, suppose that the subject is talking about her husband who was injured in an accident. When the interview is over, you can shoot a cutaway of the victim's photograph which is resting on the mantel or the desk. In the editing, while the wife speaks about her husband, the cutaway of his photo is seen, thus establishing for the viewer what the husband looks like. You should always be alert to visual possibilities beyond the limits of the interview situation itself.

There are other pictures that are extremely useful for the final editing of a story. A skilled cameraperson will be certain to shoot these without being reminded, but no reporter should take it for granted that the work has been done. The footage should be specifically requested. Most of these shots can be used for voice-overs of a general kind and therefore they are handy to have, even if you have taken other visuals that you prize more highly.

One of these pictures is a *two-shot*. A two-shot is just what it sounds like—a picture of the two people involved in the interview—the reporter and the news source. Two-shots can be used as cutaways, as bridges, and as a means to set up or lead into the interview itself.

The two-shot offers more visual flexibility than does the listening shot. A creative cameraperson can take pictures of the pair from a variety of angles. He might take a nice long shot, one that sets the scene for the interview in an interesting setting: a home, an office, a garden, against a panoramic view. A shot that is long enough to show the participants and the setting, but in which the lips cannot be seen moving, makes a nice cutaway for a change of visuals during an interview.

A *two-shot for editing:* Suppose the subject is speaking, and instead of cutting away to a listening shot of the reporter alone, you want to cut to a shot that shows the reporter listening; but you want to show the back of the subject as well. The viewer will hear the subject's voice, see his back, but also see the reporter. You will need a two-shot that shows the reporter *not speaking*. Suppose you want to cover the reporter's questions, then move back to the subject for the answer. For this particular two-shot, you will need a picture over the shoulder of the reporter, with the subject *not speaking*. These two-shots are not absolutely necessary for a story, but where you intend to use an extended interview, they can make the difference between a mediocre edited product and one that has class.

A *two-shot for a bridge or setting up an interview:* Sometimes the interview is part of a larger news package, and to set up the new scene, you will want to lead into the sound-bites with a picture of the interview setting. You may write in your voice-over bridge, "Over at City Hall, the Comptroller was saying that all these charges are false," and then come up with sound-bites of the Comptroller. You could cover this bridge with the two-shot that shows you and the comptroller talking in his paneled office. There are times when you may feel the need to do a brief voice-over bridge within the interview in order to explain or offer background to the interviewee's statements, and again the two-shot is helpful.

Just as the two-shot or long shot can set the scene for an interview, an *establishing shot* can set the scene in another kind of visual story. The establishing shot is a wide, overview picture that brings the viewer right onto the scene. It gives him a sense of place by showing where the story is occurring, its background, and its dimensions.

If you are covering a neighborhood, you might make your way on to a hill or a rooftop and then shoot down to show the character and dimensions of the area. Or you can drive slowly past the fronts of houses and stores to capture the shape and nature of the buildings, roads, trees, and signs.

In an interview, you try to show the atmosphere of the place where you and the subject are sitting—the lamps on the tables, the shape of the furniture, the wallpaper and paintings on the walls—all in one shot. Hold each shot for at least ten or twelve seconds before changing pictures. In the editing process, the shots that are finally used are normally from two to five seconds long. You can see from this that you will need a wide variety and number of shots even for a thirty- or forty-second voice-over.

Earlier you learned about the necessity for a television reporter to make quick news decisions while in the field. The point is, you need to know fairly precisely what you intend to say so that you can shoot the appropriate pictures while you are still on the scene. If you are not sure how the story will look in the end, then you should have the camera operator shoot several possible versions. It is better to have extra shots than to return without enough material to edit. Remember that ultimately the words you have on sound-bites plus the words that you write, when combined with the pictures that your crew has obtained, must convey the necessary information to tell the story.

Always shoot material that humanizes a story, especially if your script is dealing in abstractions. If you are reporting about a neighborhood, of course you will want to show houses and stores, signs and cars. But show us people walking and talking and children playing as well.

Shoot faces, a variety of faces. Shoot crowds. What you shoot should illustrate what you have to say, but it is also helpful to have general material that can be used for nonspecific voice-overs.

Sometimes you can create visual action for a story by having yourself filmed as you walk up the steps and to the door of the house where the interview is to take place. Where an interview is about a subject matter that can be illustrated, walk with the news source or shoot pictures of the individual walking alone through the relevant area—a lot, a factory, a store, a park, a hallway. In the editing process an effective technique is to use the subject's voice over pictures of him walking and showing what he is talking about. Plainly this would be of greater visual interest than a simple sit-down interview.

There is still another segment of the story that requires the attention of the reporter in the field: *the stand-up*. A stand-up is the picture in which the reporter appears on the scene, microphone in hand, and reports directly to the viewer. (Even when done while sitting, it is still called a stand-up). Here is the point in the telling of the story when the reporter is seen most clearly. Although her voice may have been heard in interviews and voice-overs, it is now that she is seen full face on camera, addressing her audience, and thus becomes a distinct personality. The stand-up stamps the story with the reporter's imprimatur.

When do you do a stand-up? A good rule is not to inject yourself into the story unless it is necessary. Where you have fine action, good interviews, let the story essentially tell itself. Some news organizations like to see the reporter in a news package, and it is not a bad idea to do a brief stand-up close. Stand-ups are also handy where you have inadequate visuals, or you are shifting scenes and need a bridge. However you plan to employ the stand-up, make sure that you choose a setting that is relevant to the story, preferably something visually interesting and dramatic.

A stand-up should not repeat what has already been said by the anchor, the voice-over, or the sound-bites. In order to avoid repeating these earlier elements, you have to know pretty well what you are going to put into the body of the story before you do your stand-up.

A stand-up should lend meaning to the story. It should put it into some kind of perspective. If the story itself tends to paint a rosy picture, your stand-up might add balance by citing direct quotes or evidence from the other side. If the story is anecdotal, representing one small part of a larger picture, then place the report in context, and relate it to the larger picture. The stand-up can report on still-unanswered questions or point out remaining loose ends. It could include a report on what is happening tomorrow, or what lies further ahead. A stand-up should never be trite, obvious, pat, or trivial. It should be substantive, meaningful, and add valuable information or insight to the total report.

The value of the stand-up is that it places the reporter on the scene, an effective way to lend credibility. The viewer accepts that the reporter was there because he can see her with his own eyes. The stand-up also introduces the viewer to the reporter's face and presence, which in effect humanizes her and to some extent reveals the nature of the person who has gathered the news. In addition, the stand-up lends a certain visible authority to the story through the visual impact of a reporter speaking face to face with the viewer. Because of the powerful impact of the reporter's presence, her writing in the stand-up must be particularly lucid and stylish. Especially is this so for the last line that is spoken into the camera. Before the sign-off, the viewer should be left with the memory of a telling phrase.

When you do a stand-up, write two or three sentences—crisp, punchy, grabby sentences—then sign off: "This is Robyn Smith at City Hall, reporting for Columbia News." Hold the microphone well below your face, at mid-chest. Do not read your notes. Memorize them. Talk conversationally into the camera. If you are unhappy with your first take, do the stand-up again and again until you are satisfied with your performance. A professional will make every effort to be seen only in a polished stand-up.

A *warning*: Never fool around on camera or use bad language, even though you do not intend for that particular take to be used on the air. It has happened on occasion that a hurried editor plucked out the wrong piece of videotape and aired it. In one case, the reporter was seen on the air using foul language. As a consequence, *the reporter* was fired for unprofessional behavior, even though it could be argued that the mistake was essentially that of the editor. Always behave as though your efforts are going out live on camera. It is not only professional, it is good discipline.

Remember, too, when you have finished your stand-up, you should remain in the same position for several seconds, until the cameraperson says "cut." This is important for the editing, since it assures that you are not seen moving away as the story ends. It also gives enough videotape padding to cover any control room mishaps that could leave your story on the air beyond its scheduled time. Your picture would be seen signing off and waiting a second or two on camera, instead of going to black.

A stand-up should be delivered in a relaxed but authoritative manner. You must imagine the lens of the camera to be a person, so that you are talking one-to-one, in a serious and intimate way. Do not shout your stand-up, even if you are standing in a noisy spot. Keep in mind that the viewer will be watching you when he is inside his house, probably sitting quietly in his living room. He will hardly appreciate being yelled at by a reporter who is in a sense a visitor to his home. If you are doing your stand-up in a place that is noisy, bring the microphone up close to your mouth and speak into it normally.

Sometimes you will find yourself working in a spot that is windy. The wind will badly affect the sound in the microphone unless the microphone is covered by a cloth or foam "wind sock." Make sure that your technician provides one to ensure good quality sound.

If you have done a stand-up in the field, but later the story changes, or you have better, later developments, then the stand-up should be dropped from the story. You should go back to the studio to do your close incorporating the latest information live on camera.

The important thing is not to be locked into the visual aspects of the story. The prime responsibility of the reporter is to tell the story accurately, fully, and in a balanced and *up-to-date* form.

Because the same news story may appear in several different broadcasts, it is important to tape different stand-ups as well as to rewrite the script. It is vital to keep in mind the time of the broadcast in which your story will appear. Thus, a morning fire that leaves ten families homeless must have a "tonight" angle for the six P.M. or especially, the 11 P.M. news program.

Even if your story is geared for only one newscast, do not be satisfied with the substance of a story shot at say, 10 A.M., for airing that evening. Check the newswires for later developments. Get on the telephone and find out if anything has happened after you and your crew left the scene. Never settle for information that is hours old. Television news in particular is a "now" medium of information, and the viewer has the right to know what is the latest news at hand.

If you are unable to appear in the studio to do a new updated close live on camera, the outdated video stand-up should still be dropped, and the new information written for delivery by the anchorperson. It is more important for the viewer to have timely and correct information than it is to see you on screen.

CHAPTER FIVE.

Packaging the Television News Story

Once the television story has been gathered and videotaped, the reporter must make plans for packaging it. In print terms, this would be called the process of writing, editing and laying out the story. When the television reporter packages, he writes the words that will cover some of the pictures, chooses those pictures, picks out the sound-bites for his story, and determines the placement for the various elements in it. He is in a sense editor, layout editor, photographic editor, as well as reporter. What he has to provide to his station for the news broadcast is a package, and the package must be complete when it is delivered.

However, you cannot shape the final package until you receive instructions from home base. When you are field reporting, you need to keep in touch with the news desk back at the station. The news director and executive producer will be trying to shape the final program for that night. To make intelligent judgments about the order in which stories will appear and how long each should be, they must know the substance of the story you have in hand and your estimate of the airtime you need to tell it. The reporter may be asked to provide an early lead-in written for the anchorperson; this material will be dictated over the telephone. The news desk can also tell you whether to return to the station to supervise the editing of the final news package or to send written editing instructions instead.

In either case, know what it is that you *believe* you have on videotape. I say "believe" because sometimes the camera operator will fail to catch wanted material, and there can also be technical failures. Keep a written record of useful material as it is taped—cover shots, cutaways, interviews, stand-ups. Indicate in your "log" of this material, roughly where it can be found on the videotape, and if you have used more than one videotape cassette, make sure that each one is numbered and indicate which material is on which cassette. Your log should state which of the stand-ups you want to be incorporated into the final story, and which specific sound-bites you want to be used.

To indicate the specific sound-bite to be included in the story, write down where the sound-bite is located and on which cassette, and then state the *in-cue* and the *out-cue* (sometimes called the *end-cue*). That is, specify the first few words of the sound-bite (in-cue) and the last few words of the sound-bite (out-cue). Thus:

MAYOR SOT:
Tape one, approximately two minutes in:
  In-cue: "He failed to support. . . .
  Out-cue: . . . to govern this city."
:15 (or 15 seconds.)

Note that at the end of this instruction you indicate the approximate length of the sound-bite. This information is helpful to the editor who may be asked by the producer to either shorten or lengthen the story, depending upon his evaluation of its worth and the needs of the program. As you grow more experienced, you will be able to make rough judgments about the length of a sound-bite even as it is being delivered by the speaker. You may also want to use a stopwatch to time the bite more accurately.

Suppose that you have in mind a fairly simple story, one that would include the following elements: anchor lead-in, reporter voice-over silent pictures, one sound-bite, and a stand-up close.

At the top of your editing instructions you put the *slug*. A slug is several words designated by the desk to identify your story. Not so long ago, a slug was one word, or at the most, two. However, as assignment desks become computerized, slugs grow longer and the computer system requires consistency in how things are slugged. Thus:

DEPUTY MAYOR RESIGNATION CITY HALL   Time: 11.45 A.M.
SMITH (reporter's name)
ANCHOR LEAD-IN: Mayor X today announced the resignation of Deputy
                     Mayor Z and the appointment of a local lawyer to take
12 seconds.   his place. Robyn Smith has more on the story.

SMITH VO/VTR: The Mayor's announcement came as no surprise. For
beginning sec-   months he has been visibly displeased with his depu-
ond tape: ty's public and private statements. Etc.
general shots,
news conference
22 seconds
MAYOR SOT: in cue: "Z failed to support. . . .
                       out cue: . . . govern this city."
tape one, about
two minutes in,
15 seconds.
SMITH SOT: in cue: "The Mayor's appointment of . . .
stand-up, take   out cue: . . . for Columbia News."
four, middle
tape two
20 seconds.

                       Total time, with anchor: 1.09.

Notice that, to the left of your rough script you are indicating the visuals
for the story, with particular attention to the visuals available for your voice-
over. The right hand side of the script indicates the spoken words. This is
the usual format of a television news script—picture instructions to the left,
words to the right.

Suppose that you are unable to return to the station in time for your story
to be edited and in time for you to record the voice-over segment. If, because of late-breaking developments, there is a chance that you cannot return to the station, you should record the voice-over portion of your script
while you are in the field. Record it on videotape, just like a stand-up, and
indicate in your editing instructions that the voice-over is on the videotape.
The editor will then lay on top of the sound of your voice the edited pictures
that are relevant to the script. If you can manage to do this on a regular
basis—that is, record your voice-over in the field—you will make the editor
and the program's producer exceedingly happy, because all the elements of
the package will be in-house early. That will relieve the pressures on editors
and facilities as the later deadlines approach.

Obviously, this kind of purposeful discipline takes time to acquire. At the
network level, most reporters are expected to report, write, and package swiftly

and effectively, although the networks also tend to leave much of the detailed editing to their in-house producers.

What you rarely have in the television news business is time to waffle over the composition of your story. Remember that what you shoot, write, and report today has to go on the air that very evening, so that the deadline pressures are constant and great. You may hunger for more time to reexamine the videotape, to reconsider the most artistic way to design your story, but in daily TV news reporting, you rarely are given that luxury.

The story described above is obviously fast-paced—too much so for the significance of the event itself. Each element of the package is brief—22 seconds, 15 seconds, 20 seconds. A story like that has *pacing*, that is, it does not dwell for too long on a single visual or aural element. The story hits the headlines in brief wham-bang style, but it offers little in the way of explanation or depth.

When packaging a TV news story, it is important to reach a balance between the demands of good journalism and the pacing demands of the television medium. Each news organization has its own style. Some like stories that are ninety seconds long and will frown on any report that is longer. These are likely to be Action News stations, tabloids of the air, wedded to a fast and snappy kind of television journalism. Other stations accept a more leisurely pace, especially where they have two hour newscasts to fill and the particular story and material merit more time. Again, you have to adapt your work to the standards of the organization that hires you.

You are going to hear a great deal about pacing in television; it is a factor that you simply cannot ignore. The medium has intrinsic requirements of time, mood, and movement, and if you fail to understand these, you run the risk of producing dull and lifeless stories. True, there are exceptions to these requirements. There are times when a sound-bite is so exciting and even magesterial that it can be allowed to run longer than the standard, and in fact it *should*. Major events like the funeral of a president, or speeches of special significance, are carried at considerable length because of their inherent interest and significance. However here we are addressing the usual demands within commercial news organizations. These concepts are neither arbitrary nor trivial, but rather grow out of experience in the medium, and the constant testing of its limits and potentialities.

How long should a sound-bite be? The shorter the better. If the news subject targets the essence in ten or twelve seconds of crisp, bright, eloquent language, then use that particular bite. The more that you deal with video-tape, the quicker you will learn to recognize that most people use words in a flabby and obfuscating way, and that much of the point and intent of speech can be summed up succinctly. As you begin to package a story, you should search through your material and reach for the "moment of truth," then STOP. Often the hardest decision is to know when to stop. What you are looking for in a sound-bite is impact—*depth* instead of *length*.

Each of the elements in a news story should not be allowed to drag on. A voice-over should be about twenty to thirty seconds long, depending on the length of the cuts of the videotape and the power of the visuals. You can create pacing by cutting pictures of two or three seconds in length, giving the effect of a kaleidoscope. However, even with the liveliest of visuals, you should avoid talking "at" your viewers for too long a time. Break up your narrative with sound-bites. Furthermore, you should use the sound-bites to *tell* the story, not just to support or amplify what you have written.

For example, in a particular story you might write twenty seconds of voice-over narration, then move to a sound-bite of fifteen seconds, to voice-over of ten seconds, and then to three sound-bites of twelve, ten, and fifteen seconds, one following the other in quick procession. You would wrap it all up with a stand-up of twelve seconds. Each change from one kind of segment to another gives a sense of movement, action, and pacing. The effect is that of a montage. However, care must be exercised when choosing these clips, so that they make sense by relating to each other in a rational way.

From the above it is plain that television puts a premium on tight, bright, pithy writing. You are going to have to learn to say a great deal in a few words and to choose what to say with unerring aim. There will be a later chapter on writing for television news, but it can be said here that the art of writing for TV is a highly skilled, precision form of communication. In the hands of a talented writer, the pictures develop meanings of enormous power and persuasion.

When you package a television news story, you are exercising a creative judgment that in effect imposes your intelligence on the story. You have to judge fairly early what is extraneous or expendable and what fails to go to the central point of the story. Sometimes you have material that is spicy or jazzy on your videotape, and you are tempted to use it because it is there—

maybe just because it is there. Resist! You have a story to tell—a news story—and while you have to tell it vividly, you should not skew the journalism to suit a lively piece of videotape. *Always* set the journalistic priority above any demand for gratuitous drama and excitement.

When you are doing a stand-up in the field, the sound quality of your voice will be quite different from the quality achieved when you read a script in the studio. For one thing, the field stand-up may have street noises or other background noises behind you, while the studio narrative will be pristine. Wherever possible, then, you should try not to butt a soundtrack of your voice in the field against a soundtrack of your voice in the studio. The shift can be distracting. One way to overcome this problem is to write your entire script in the field, and read it as a stand-up. Part of your stand-up will appear with you on camera, but the rest of it will be used as a voice-over, with pictures edited to cover that part of your script.

The use of *B-roll* is one of the more creative ornaments available for the packaging of a story. In effect, the A-roll is where the sound is. The B-roll gives you the option of laying pictures over the sound shot in the field. These terms come from film rather than videotape. With film, you literally have two separate rolls on two separate reels, and they are marked A and B. With videotape, the entire process is laid down on a single piece of tape.

However, the goal is the same. For example, suppose that you have some excellent sound-bites from an interview, but the speaker is not too exciting and the visuals are rather dull. You could allow the speaker to talk (on the A-roll) for awhile, with his face showing to establish who he is. Then, while continuing the sound of his voice, you lay over (on B-roll) pictures of what he is talking about. This technique improves the pacing because it offers visual change. It also supports the basic idea that in television it is often better to show something than to talk about it.

In other words, where you can illustrate the speaker's point, do so. You may only want to give a sense of place or establish a mood. It is still a useful device. The person interviewed is talking, and while you hear his voice, you see him strolling in his garden or climbing stairs or doing something else that is active and that shows where he lives and what he does. The words are enhanced by the pictures.

As a reporter in a professional news organization, it is unlikely that you will be called on to physically edit your videotape. However, you are normally expected to field produce and to package your own stories, with the help of an editor. Where you are blessed with the aid of a creative editor, give him something of a free hand in the *design* of the package, subject of course to your editorial direction and control. As a reporter, you are not expected to be so skilled in the art of visual continuity as a talented editor would be. Nevertheless it is useful for you to be aware of the various alternative ways that you can design a story and remain open to suggestions that could improve on your original ideas for the package. You can learn a great deal simply by critically watching television news programs, examining the ways that stories are assembled and judging what seems to work well and what does not.

For example, suppose that you want to use a number of sound-bites in your story, a kind of point-counterpoint argument between one speaker and another. Suppose in the story cited above you have a sound-bite from the Mayor, then a sound-bite from the deputy who resigned, and then a piece from the new deputy; and you want to use all of them in your story. In fact, considering the nature of that story, it is advisable that you do so, to give the resigning deputy a chance to defend himself and his replacement a chance to explain how her arrival is likely to change the situation.

If airtime is limited, you can save vital seconds by avoiding the necessity to introduce each speaker separately. Simply cut from the Mayor to the resigning deputy to the new person, abutting one sound-bite against another. In order to identify each speaker, you use what is called a *super.* The name of the speaker and his identification are superimposed in letters at the bottom of the picture. This is done from the control room, as the program is on the air. If you intend to use supers, indicate on the script the name and identity of each speaker in order, and mark these items SUPER. Moving directly from one sound-bite to another is an excellent way to employ pacing, without in any way losing the meaning of a story.

Perhaps you have a story that involves stunning action or deep emotion. You may choose to open your package using the heart of the action, with the sound full up. Natural sound can be a dramatic kind of opening, bringing the viewer right into the story before the reporter launches his explanation of what the story is about. After the natural sound, the reporter follows with his narrative voice-over, but this time his voice does not cover *silent* pictures. Instead his narrative is heard over what is called *half-track.* The narrative runs against the background of the natural sound played at reduced volume.

For example, suppose that you have covered a lively demonstration. During the march, there were several moments of chanting or prayer that clearly reveal and epitomize the mood of the event. Instead of opening your story with your voice-over pictures, explaining the event, you begin with a few seconds of untouched natural sound-with-picture—the few moments that capsulize the drama of the event.

Then, the pictures continue, with the natural sound now lowered in volume to play behind your voice-over narrative in which you proceed to explain what the viewer has just been witnessing. With this technique, you are letting the story tell itself without interference, bringing the viewer directly into the event before you begin to report on it.

The key to good packaging is to be alert to the visual and dramatic possibilities of the television story, just as you need to be alert to an exciting news lead for a print story. But again, avoid the temptation to let the dramatic tail wag the journalistic dog. Use dramatic material only when it is plainly relevant to the news story.

CHAPTER SIX.

The "Tell" Story

The tell story is a story reported without visuals. Few television stations own enough cameras to send one out on every story, and not every story needs pictures. Therefore, the reporter will be expected at times to cover an event without a camera crew, to write a script and then read it on the air.

Sometimes the reporter will videotape his presentation in advance of the program. More likely he will be reading his script live from the studio news set.

If you happen to see yourself primarily as a writer, and you have at times, even secretly, resented the way that the demands of videotape tend to take over a television story, you will probably welcome the chance to do tell stories. They offer a challenge to your writing abilities and a special opportunity to exercise your talents in that direction.

The tell story appears to be simple and easy. It is not. For one thing, most are brief, a mere forty-five seconds to one minute long, compared with a videotaped report that can run to two or two and a half minutes. The videotaped story includes the attraction of the "direct quotes" of sound-bites as well as the liveliness and interest of pictures. The tell story relies entirely on the ability of the reporter to write succinctly and vividly, and to transmit the story using only his personal credibility and on-air delivery.

Given the brevity of the report, every line in the tell story must count. Necessary information has to be provided if the viewer is going to understand what you are saying. However, anything that is a digression or is irrelevant has to be discarded. The story can contain no clutter. It must be lean, precise, and colorfully written. If you write or talk in a wooden, plodding fashion, you will lose your viewing audience.

Keep the story simple. Avoid going into too many details. Hit the highlights only. Support the central theme.

Humor helps if it is in keeping with the story. A witty line, a telling phrase, presented with a sparkle in the reporter's eye, can be very effective.

Keep your sentences short and punchy. They will be easier to read and deliver on the air. You should clearly mark out the beginning of each sentence so that you do not lose your place when you are reading.

Rehearse your script. If you have trouble delivering a line, change it. Some writing looks fine in print, but it simply does not work for broadcasting. The tell story consistently tests that principle.

Do not be afraid to use a direct quote, if the quote is short and colorful and it lends liveliness to your report. Even though you do not have videotape of the news source speaking you can use his words to humanize your story. Either paraphrase what he said or use direct quotes.

To handle direct quotes in broadcasting, you have to remember that the listener cannot see the quotation marks written on your script. You have to find a way to let the listener know that you are quoting directly and to indicate clearly where the quote begins and ends.

Some people use "quote" and "unquote" but this is a clumsy and not particularly natural way of solving your problem. Here are some phrases that you can use when dealing with direct quotes in a tell story:

- in his words.
- as he put it.
- he said, and this is a direct quote.
- he said, and we quote him.
- as he said.
- he put it this way.

In addition, the inflection of your voice can indicate to the viewer when you are quoting directly. One good way to eliminate confusion is to avoid lengthy quotes. If you have to use a long quote, break it up into separate sentences. You can use the following devices:

- he concluded by saying.
- he added this comment.

• he went on to say.
• he continues.
• he continued in these words.

An effective way to end a tell story is to use a pithy quote for the ending. For example, you lay out the story, one side and then another, and close your story this way: "Senator Markham sums it up in these words: 'No matter which way we go on this, we're in trouble.' This is Robyn Smith reporting."

Your first line and your last line are extremely important in a tell story. Your opening line should be vivid and lively, and where possible you should have it memorized. You memorize the line so that when the red light on the camera blinks on, your head will be up, your eyes alert and ready to communicate, and the words will flow out easily and directly before you have to look down at your script for your next line.

The opening line should set the mood for what will follow, or give some idea of the significance of the information you have gathered. It ought to have a news angle that will grab the viewer and hold his attention. You have to persuade the viewer to stay with you when he might otherwise be inclined to depart for the kitchen and get a beer. He is used to watching moving pictures, but the only picture on the screen is you sitting still. If your tell story lacks intrinsic value and your writing and delivery are plodding, do not expect the viewer to stay around to watch.

As a new reporter, you may feel intimidated by the prospect of writing an on-camera piece and delivering it live. Don't worry. Stage nerves are a common complaint of television reporters as well as other public performers.

One way to overcome nervousness is to put yourself in an appropriate frame of mind. Try to imagine that the red light on the studio camera is your best friend. Write the story, and later deliver it, to that individual you imagine to be sitting on the other side of the camera. This will help with your on-air delivery. It will also help you to avoid pompous or murky writing. Relate your story in a direct, intimate and conversational manner. When you look into the camera, you have to believe that it is not a camera at all, not a dead object like a stone or a building, but something alive. If you look and see only a dead camera, your eyes will develop a glazed look that can set up a barrier between you and the viewer. However, if you can see a living viewer in your mind's eye and speak *to* him instead of *at* him, you will find the right tone for reaching him.

To help put yourself at ease on camera, wherever possible allow yourself enough time to rehearse. If you can find a quiet corner to read aloud, that's fine. A good place to rehearse is in front of the bathroom mirror, even if the bathroom is a public place at the television station. You may have to rehearse at your desk in the newsroom, but you should not feel embarrassed by that. As airtime approaches in most television operations, you will find numbers of reporters seated at their desks, babbling to themselves as they rehearse their scripts. You'll be too busy to notice what your colleagues are doing, and they'll be too busy to worry about you.

Underline the words on your script that you plan to emphasize when you are reading. Write a large apostrophe at the end of phrases where you plan to pause for breath. Mark up pronunciation of words or names that could possibly cause you to trip on your tongue when you are reading. Make sure that your script is clean and legible, and if it is not, retype it. You may want to type in capitals so that the words on the page will be large and easy to read. Plan to deliver portions of the script in such a way that you will be able to maintain eye contact with the camera for long periods. Look down, memorize the next phrase or short sentence quickly, then look up and address your viewer.

At most stations, the anchorperson uses a TelePrompTer but there may not be time to include your script, particularly in the case of a late-breaking story. However, if you can arrange it, it is wise to have your script on the TelePrompTer. The prompter allows you to read your script more naturally, with your eyes looking forward into the camera instead of looking down at the printed page.

However, when you use a TelePrompTer, you have to avoid the appearance of reading in the camera. Keep your eyes and your head from swinging back and forth as you scan the copy. Blink on occasion. Avoid staring. Try to deliver the copy as though you are not reading, but speaking off the cuff. The aim is to appear natural and not frozen. The prompter is a marvelous tool when used properly and the reporter who has access to one can enhance his ability to communicate effectively. One of the most skillful users of the TelePrompTer is Alistair Cooke, host of the PBS series *Masterpiece Theater*. His easy and natural performance is a masterpiece of theater in its own right.

When you return to the studio to report live on the set, work closely with the producer and the anchorperson to make sure that the anchor's written lead-in does not conflict with or involve repetition of your material. Furthermore, take care to reserve some significant information for follow-up discussion with the anchor, if that kind of follow-up is planned. Anchor–reporter exchanges on the set can highlight a significant story, and they give the reporter an opportunity to explain in more detail the background and meaning of a developing story.

CHAPTER SEVEN.

Working Live

Television is remarkable in its ability to bring us an event as it is happening. When a President is inaugurated, when a Watergate committee holds hearings, when a football game is in progress, we can sit at home and watch the event unfold before our eyes. Electronic News Gathering, or ENG, has made that possible. Broadcasting is the medium of "now." The sense of immediacy gives the medium much of its power and attractiveness in a society that enjoys pursuing what is latest and newest. Aside from the heightened sense of participation that the live report offers to the viewer, immediacy has its journalistic value. When something of importance occurs, like the attempted assassination of a President, it is useful for the citizen to receive that information promptly, since the fate of his government hangs on the outcome of the event.

However, the problem with television's instant technology is that the pictures are often transmitted before the supportive information can be checked for accuracy, and before background material can be made available. We see *something*, but we don't necessarily know or understand what it is. Pictures unaccompanied by appropriate explanation can be misleading.

In March 1981, when John W. Hinckley Jr. fired in the direction of President Ronald Reagan, videotape cameras captured the scene, but the pictures alone failed to reveal that the President had been wounded. Early reports indicated that the President had escaped unscathed—and in fact Ronald Reagan himself did not realize he had been hit. The networks played and replayed the startling pictures of the shooting scene, but their meaning remained unclear until the basic reporting and verification from the hospital could be done.

Early reports that the President's press secretary, James Brady, had died of his wounds, were instantly transmitted, only to be corrected later when they were found to be inaccurate. Going live with a breaking story can be a journalist's nightmare.

In spite of the obvious risks, local stations now use live reports on a regular basis. Many stations have invested millions of dollars in minicams, or action cams—videotape units connected to a van or a truck, which can beam an event directly back to the station. This marvel of modern technology is enormously valuable when there is a story or event worthy of such treatment, but extraordinary events do not occur every day. Most of what is newsworthy and reportable requires patient checking, careful weighing of evidence, and rational ordering of material. Most of all, it requires time for reflection.

What live television does not allow is time for reflection, for second thoughts. The reporter has to "go with what he's got," right there, on the spot. He cannot delete unimportant material, nor does he have the opportunity to reshape the material to improve its form and logic. When he ad libs, he may choose the wrong word, misstate some facts, leave out important information. A story presented live, without benefit of editing or editor, can quite easily slip from the reporter's control.

There are two schools of thought on the merits of presenting material live and unedited to the viewing public. One side argues that this offers the citizen the chance to see the story whole and unchanged by the reporter's interventions. What happens happens, and the reporter's only role is to be the vehicle for gathering the information on the scene. The viewer sees the raw material as it is gathered. He is spared the point-of-view refinements inherent in the packaging and processing of that raw material.

Critics, on the other hand, view this kind of television news as an abdication of the journalist's responsibility to provide shape and meaning to events. For example, the typical live interview offers the person interviewed the opportunity to manipulate the occasion to his own advantage. He can filibuster, or expound on issues unrelated to the question asked. He can grandstand. He can even be offensive, if he so chooses. He knows that what he is saying will not be edited, and that gives to him a power that preferably should remain in the hands of the reporter—the power to control the situation. The short, live, field interview rarely allows the reporter time to challenge a statement, seek out verification, or even to balance the live interview with opposing views. Much journalistic integrity is sacrificed in order to go live, be first, and talk now.

One can argue that when the story assigned is significant and clearly merits live coverage, the reporter has substantive material to deal with. What he reports now is important and timely, and therefore he may be forgiven for certain shortcomings in the quality of the reporting. However, much of the live reporting done on local television is hardly worth the tradeoff. Again and again, presumably serious reporters are seen reporting live from the scene of events that occurred hours earlier, or about stories that are only marginally newsworthy. The reporter who might better be spending his time checking sources and updating his story is instead shipped off to some now-vacant streetcorner so that he can appear live on camera.

This attraction for live coverage stems in part from the perception that it gives the public the feeling that it is participating in something as it happens. There is also the realization that stations have invested more than forty thousand dollars for each minicam, and that enormous investment in technology has to be justified.

It is plain that the television reporter who works live from the field has to have skills that go beyond the basic ones required for pre-taped stories, or for live tell stories in the studio. The tell story is written and scripted after the reporter has absorbed the material, mulled it over in his mind, and set it down on paper. It will have been written, rewritten, and edited before it goes on air. But the reporter working live without a script cannot reevaluate information, redirect the original thrust of the story, or tighten up the language. He has one chance at it. The material is expected to be delivered accurately, logically, clearly—and instantly.

The necessary skills can be developed in time, but they have to rest on a firm foundation. You need a finely honed sense of what is and is not important, what is and is not news, and the limits of good taste. You must exercise control over your emotions and keep tight rein on your biases. You should have a keen eye for the details of what is happening, and the ability to make swift, analytical judgments about the patterns and significance of that information. You have to be cautious in your reporting; say only the things that you know to be true, and qualify any reports that are doubtful or have not been adequately verified. You need to remain serene, even when the events around you are dangerous or chaotic. The ethical underpinnings of your work as a journalist will help to keep you in balance and in control under the severe test of live reporting only if the controls are strong and running on automatic.

The live interview in the field can reveal starkly the quality of mind that you bring to your work. A banal question cannot be edited out; it hangs in the air for all the world to hear and see. Since there is no opportunity to edit, your capacity to listen to answers, to follow up, and to probe, is laid bare. Many live interviews are superficial "man-on-the-streets," or are about frivolous topics. You'll be expected to come up with the colorful characters and lively commentary from the public, without turning yourself into a clown. This is not an easy thing to do when the story assignment is insubstantial. However, it helps enormously if you genuinely like people, and maintain a sense of humor.

Who decides what stories will go live? Sometimes it is the assignment editor, who may also be called the electronic news coordinator. More often than not it is the executive producer. An important breaking story will naturally lead to live coverage, although events like riots are videotaped in order to maintain control over the material and avoid inflaming the public. Sometimes the decision to go live has nothing much to do with the intrinsic value of a story. The producer may feel that the program is shaping up as too serious, and he believes that the injection of a live-from-the-field report will add zest and vitality to the program.

When you are out in the field, you keep in touch with the station by means of two-way radio. When on air, you wear an earpiece, through which you obtain instructions from the producer. Sometimes the producer will suggest lines of questioning or give you information on another story that is relevant to the event that you are covering.

The reporter who is working live is expected to look amiably into the camera or to conduct an interview, even as he is receiving assorted directions, queries, and promptings through his earpiece. It takes a certain kind of coolness under fire to pull this act off, because the aim is to keep the viewer unaware of the vexatious drumbeat in the reporter's ear even as he reports on camera. Amidst the general chatter, the producer gives the reporter his cues, indicating when to start and when to wind up. There are times when the anchorperson in the studio will ask questions of the reporter in the field. All of these interconnections add the sense of now-ness that television values. They also add to the stress of the job.

A common practice in television is to combine the live report with voice-over, pre-taped material. The reporter is live on the scene, presenting the latest news, and then he leads to his own, pre-taped voice-over showing the events that occurred earlier. At the end the camera returns to the reporter as he concludes his remarks live.

What happens is this: when the visuals are videotaped earlier in the day, they are beamed directly back to the station, where they are edited. The reporter can either pre-record the voice-over on videotape, or read it live from the field while the station runs the videotape on the air. The combined live and videotaped story has the merit of showing the reporter on the scene while he brings the story up to date. In addition, the earlier visual material offers the background of events leading up to this moment.

A typical story covered in this fashion would be the negotiations between the city and its transit workers union to end a transportation strike. You have been covering the story as it unfolds during the day, showing the impact of the strike on commuter traffic, interviewing negotiators as they come and go, trying to determine what issues are at stake and where the negotiations are heading. Later that evening, in your live report, still at the scene of the negotiations, you report, perhaps, that a final agreement is imminent.

Having reported the breaking news live, you then lead to a voice-over of the earlier, edited, taped story, to explain how the strike affected the city and the progress of the negotiations throughout the day. This is a superb use of television's capacity to go live, since it gives the viewer the information he needs immediately, but it also gives him the background to understand what led up to the events that are occurring now. The report combines substance with immediacy.

There are times when you may be expected to fill in as the anchor for a program, and therefore you would be wise to prepare yourself for this eventuality. Some anchors are merely presenters or script readers. Their news copy is written for them. However, most anchorpersons write a considerable amount of the copy that they are to deliver on the air, and they even work with the producer in deciding how to lead the program and shape the final product.

The qualities required of a good anchorperson are authority, believability, warmth, coolness under fire, a gift for humor, serenity, friendly appearance, clear-spoken. However, some of these qualities are difficult to define. What appears authoritative to one viewer may strike another one as pompous. One person's perceived warmth is interpreted as frostiness by another. What is humorous to me may seem silly to you. The viewing audience is as diverse in its judgments as it is in its tastes.

There are limits to how much a reporter can do to turn himself into anchor material, but he can work with whatever nature gave him as a start. Here are a few tips:

• Spruce up your appearance. Try a strict diet, a good haircut, and simple clothes.

• Practice your on-air delivery before an off-air camera. Then critically appraise the videotape that is played back to you.

• Consciously eliminate such mannerisms as frowning or licking your lips.

• Apply makeup to cover up distracting blemishes and to emphasize your better features.

• Practice the art of writing scripts that are bright, lively, and flow smoothly from the lips.

• Work on your use of the TelePrompTer. Read copy without visibly swinging your eyes back and forth. Do not stare. Blink naturally now and then. Read *to* the camera, not *at* it.

• Practice reading from a script so that you can be looking up for much of the time. Eye contact is important. If your eyes are glued to the page, the viewer will see only the top of your head, and that makes communicating difficult.

• The floor manager in the studio is the person who indicates to you which camera you should be looking into. Make sure you understand his signals and follow them.

• Develop a technique for leading gracefully into a piece of videotape. Some anchors will turn to look at the monitor, and the camera will be on them as they watch the next tape come up. You should decide in advance how you want to handle this task.

• Think through what you will do if things go wrong. Practice the art of graceful recovery. That is, how to turn a technical failure or on-air blooper into a moment of no, or light consequence.

In addition to reading news stories and introducing live and videotaped reports, the anchorperson may be expected to engage in chit-chat with the co-anchor, the sports man or the weather man, and do live on-air interviews with news sources in the studio or with reporters in the field. For any of these assignments the anchorperson has to bring his total self—his values, ethics, education, intellect, worldview, and sense of humor.

Newcomers to television sometimes make the mistake of projecting their voices on the news set as though they were on stage. Remember that television is an intimate, one-on-one medium and you should speak as you would to another person who is in the same room with you. Imagine that the camera is a living person and tell your stories to that person. Keep the pitch of your voice down, but avoid a monotone. Read the copy emphasizing the appropriate words and phrases and read as though it had real meaning for you, a meaning you want very much to share. Make sure that your face reflects the meanings you are delivering. Avoid smiling if the story is tragic and do not shake your head or commiserate either. The newsperson's job is to tell the story objectively and coolly. The anchorperson in particular has to project this sense of distance and calm, even when the events he is reporting are dramatic and frightening.

While each word should be clearly understood, avoid reading with exaggerated diction. The words should flow out naturally and easily in a conversational, not oratorical, fashion. You can improve your reading skills by working with audio tape, recording your voice, listening critically, and then re-reading the news copy until you sound the way you want to sound.

Some people become anchors on the basis of natural gifts. But even these fortunate individuals have to learn the specific techniques of anchoring. For those others who need to apply practice and some artifice in order to become acceptable anchor material, there is no substitute for hard work, persistence, and the capacity to honestly assess, criticize, and improve your own work.

News Producer Phil Metlin surrounded by the material a news producer needs to formulate an actual news program: scripts, wire material, log sheets for videotape, a calculator, phones and a typewriter.

The news program now originates from the newsroom rather than a studio. Two small ENG-type cameras are used, although the cameras carry TelePrompTer devices so that the anchorpersons can maintain eye contact with the camera while reading the script. The anchors are Hank Baughman and Jane Crawford, who do the 6 and 11 P.M. news at WPXI in Pittsburgh.

News Director Kenneth Tiven (1) confers with reporter Judie Fertig regarding a script for the 5:30 live news program. The organization of the news program is clearly displayed on a large board behind them. Reporters' scripts are read carefully for content, accuracy, and how they are visually put together. After a script is "cleared" the reporter joins a videotape editor to put it together for the program.

Executive Producer Robert Reichblum confers with the Control Room while anchors Hank Baughman and Jane Crawford do the newscast from the newsroom.

While weatherman Pat Finn delivers the forecast, a producer works on last minute stories and the Executive Producer minds the store. Finn is delivering the weather in front of a shade that allows for the Chromakey matting of his picture and computerized weather maps. When not in use the shade disappears into the woodwork, above.

Anchoring from the newscenter. The TelePrompTer person is in the far background feeding copies of the script.

Floor Manager Andy Sohngen prepares to cue the anchor who is talking with Sports Reporter DeHaven Thompson.

CHAPTER EIGHT.

The Art of Reporting for Television

There are two basic missions in reporting. One is the gathering of information. The other is shaping that information into a rational journalistic whole.

It is the morning of a working day at a local television station. You are a new reporter and you are assigned to cover a story. Your assignment editor will have heard about the story from any of a number of sources. It may be a planned event listed in the UPI or AP daybook. Someone could have phoned the news desk to alert the station that the event would be occurring. Advance notice could have come in a news release (a "handout") from a government, private industry, or public interest source. Perhaps you are being asked to follow up on a story that was reported in this morning's newspaper or to find a local angle to a national story moving on the newswires.

However your news desk learned about the story, it is up to you to find out all you can before you travel to the scene to cover it. Ask your assignment editor for printed material, telephone contacts, or background information that is at hand. Search your mind for tips, connections or sources that could give you background information or direct help. Make telephone calls to people involved in the story or who may have expertise on the subject.

It is unlikely that your news organization will have a morgue—a library of newspaper clippings—but you may be able to use the one at the local newspaper office. How much you are able to do before you go out with your crew will depend on the time that is available before the event is scheduled to occur.

If you are "flying-blind," that is, you know next-to-nothing about the subject, personalities, and issues involved, then you should ask your assignment editor to give you a "fill," that is, to sketch out the background to the story and to indicate what he or she has in mind. It is perfectly proper to seek guidance from the editor when you know yourself to be weak in a particular subject matter.

Unfortunately some assignment editors have only vague notions about the details or substance of the story they are assigning. Under pressure to provide sufficient stories to fill the time for that evening's newscast and in order to keep reporters and cameras occupied, your editor may be sending you to an event about which he has insubstantial knowledge.

Do you have the right to go to a TV news story and report back that there was nothing newsworthy happening? In theory, you do. However in most local operations, if you are assigned to cover a story and a camera crew has been committed to it, you are expected to come through with a videotaped report just the same. In effect, your mission is to take any assignment, no matter how vague and unpromising, and translate it into a story that is worth telling. Many a sow's ear has been turned into a silk purse by perceptive reporting, witty writing, and creative packaging. *Big* news the story may not be, but it will fill its allotted time slot on the evening news program and maybe even manage to bring an amused chuckle or light relief to the viewer.

A practical piece of advice for the new television reporter is this: avoid grizzling and grumping, no matter what is assigned to you. Attack each assignment with cheerfulness and willingness, even though it may look like a time-waster and a bore. Much of news in any day and in whatever medium is routine and even dull. If you can master the art of taking what is routine and dull and turning it into something lively and interesting, you will be highly prized as a television reporter. However, it all begins with the right approach to the story—the appropriate mindset.

For example: A Washington television reporter was assigned to cover the story of a confirmation hearing on Capitol Hill that was supposed to result in political fireworks. As it turned out, the fireworks were never lit. The Senators who were expected to vigorously cross-examine the nominee were instead lobbing pussycat questions in his direction. The crowd that came to watch began to thin out early, and even the nominee's wife was observed nodding sleepily in her chair. What had been billed as a lively Senatorial challenge to the President's choice for a Cabinet post turned instead into a love-fest.

How did she tell that particularly desultory story for the television audience? She asked the cameraman to turn his camera away from the Senators and the nominee and to focus instead on the spectators. There the camera captured pictures of the nominee's wife struggling to keep her eyes open, a snoring *New York Times* reporter, and assorted citizens and officials yawning and napping.

The story then was told as it happened: the failure of the promised fireworks to explode, the easy questions by the Senators (with an explanation why: the nominee was a retiring member of the Congressional "club," and was therefore treated gently by his colleagues) and then, at the end, pictures of the reality of the confirmation hearings—heads nodding, eyes closed, people yawning and dozing. What had started out as an uneventful, even boring event turned into an amusing story, and a story with a journalistic point.

It is true that, had the fireworks occurred, the strong challenge and frank reply between Senators and nominee would have produced a more newsworthy story. The televised report would have given to the public some insight into the nominee's positions on issues that would confront him as a member of the President's Cabinet. But, since the verbal exchanges failed to take place, what was revealed by the reporter's story was something different: the way that Congressmen tend to protect one of their own even when they disagree sharply with his policy positions.

It would have been easy in a story like this for the reporter to head for the phone and tell the news desk that there was no story because nothing happened. But in this case, the reporter perceived that under the surface calm something ironic and reportable was happening after all.

There are other ways that this particular story could have been reported. The reporter might have moved her camera into the hallway outside of the hearing room—a "stakeout"—and, when the hearings ended, she could have invited the nominee to step before the camera to answer questions that either were not raised or remained unanswered inside of the hearing room. If sufficient air time were allowed for this particular assignment, the reporter could have indicated the nature of the confirmation hearings with the videotape, and then, working live in studio, she could have summed up with a list of the crucial questions that were not raised by the Senators. She might also have reported on the nominee's previously stated positions on relevant issues, thus providing information that had not emerged during the actual event.

These examples illustrate that when a reporter is determined to find a story, she is likely to find one. The story that appears to be a non-story is a challenge to her enterprise and persistence.

Where local television news differs from print is in the general expectation that a story covered on that day will appear on the air that same evening. Many local stations have too few reporters, and as a result each reporter can be expected to produce one, two, or three stories for the program every evening. On a slow news day, a newspaper can draw on wire services and other "fill" material to make sure that there are no blank spots on its pages. By contrast local television news operations have little local material to fall back on. The demand to fill a preselected and allotted timespan with local material gathered that same day can place a heavy burden on the individual reporter to produce a story from every assignment.

In recent years, however, local stations that are affiliated with networks receive non-local material on newsfeeds late in the afternoon. Other sources of news are satellite and cable systems. As a result of the availability of this more plentiful fill material and perceptible improvements in the quality of the stories on the newsfeeds, an increasing number of editors are able to fill their programs with features while their reporters are freed from the daily grind. Thus the reporter can spend more time on a particular story, and delay the time when it will be delivered on the air.

Running counter to this positive trend, however, is the perception of some local news managements that their reporters are performers or personalities first, and journalists second. Since management has made a heavy financial investment in a reporter, it sees distinct advantages in having that "performer" appear on camera every night. In fact, some reporters feel slighted if they are not on the program with steady regularity, and will happily forswear the benefits of delaying a story in order to make regular nightly appearances.

To return to the problems facing you on your first reporting assignment: Armed with whatever information you could elicit in advance, you and your crew travel to the site where the event is to take place. As you travel, you should discuss with the crew what the story is likely to be, and engage them in the process of determining what elements will be needed to tell the story effectively. You should seek their help in capturing the images and sounds that will complement and support the story as you expect it to develop. All of this pre-planning is done with the clear proviso that the story may turn out to be quite different from what you expect, and that you and the crew have to remain alert to unexpected developments and be prepared to change course accordingly.

You should be particularly alert to efforts by some politicians, interest groups, and demonstrators to play to your camera, that is, to perform in such a way that it makes "good television." Outrageous language, shouting, fist-shaking, name-calling—all are tactics used by people who believe that making it on television news depends on noisy and dramatic presentation. These are commonly used techniques to persuade you to tell the story the way that the "dramatic actors" want it to be told. While your mind has to remain open to the unexpected and the dramatic, at the same time you have to apply skepticism when it is apparent that you are being manipulated.

Suppose that a political figure uses the occasion of a news conference to make dramatic, emotionally charged attacks on an opponent. You can videotape the charges and make them the substance of your story. Or you can use the occasion to pose a few questions of your own—questions that challenge the politician's legislative record or actions. You have to decide whether he is going to use you to get his attack on the air (unchallenged), or whether you are going to take the opportunity to press him to answer questions on other subjects. The problems that confront you here are several. If the politician's charges are followed by concrete substantiation, that is, if his presentation is not just an effort to make public waves, then you may want to go with it as a valid story. You would then have to give the opponent a chance to reply, on videotape if he is available for cameras, in a telephone interview from which you quote his response if he is not.

However, it may be that this is a public figure who is himself the target of investigation or challenge. What he is trying to do on this particular occasion is deflect the spotlight from himself by designing a highly emotional show on issues that are either unrelated or subsidiary. What the reporter must do is evaluate the story as it is happening before his eyes, judging whether this is a clever dodge or the real thing. A useful and instructive technique is to ask a series of follow-up questions, to press the speaker to provide facts to support his position, and to turn the event back toward the central issues.

Public figures are normally unhappy when faced with this kind of maverick reporter. They call a news conference because they want their story to be told, and to be told in the way that they choose to tell it—no more, no less. Reporters who use the occasion to challenge statements and to redirect the thrust of the news conference are rarely popular, but they may get a better story in the end.

A reporter is not a stenographer. It is not his job to mindlessly swallow whatever he is told and then report it without question and without challenge. He must apply to every assignment and circumstance a judgment on a matter's significance, whether it represents reality or mere show, whether there is sufficient evidence to back up what is being said and done; in sum whether what is going on here is worth reporting.

The television story of an official's *unsubstantiated* statements at a press conference could be told this way: The official tells his story or makes his charges in his own way. The reporter then follows the sound-bite by indicating in voice-over or a stand-up where the holes in the case are, or where the official failed to back up his statement with evidence. In this way, the reporter places the story in context and serves the public's need to understand and evaluate the event. The politician speaks his piece, and the reporter appends a rider: "yes—*but.*"

In sum, the responsibility of the reporter is not merely to say "this happened," but "this happened and this is how it happened, this is why it happened, and these are the questions that remain unanswered." For this kind of journalism, the reporter has to be well-read, intelligent, thoughtful, and skeptical. He must impose his intelligence on the material being gathered, and give it shape and order even when the event itself offers a jumble of chaotic ideas and impressions.

Does the reporter's effort change the nature of the event itself? Indeed it does. The reporter reaches for objectivity by being accurate, fair, and balanced in his presentation. But what he sees, what he chooses out of the welter of material to raise to significance, how he shapes the story in words, pictures, and the edited package—all of these are subjective judgments.

Journalism is a profession, and professionals are expected to exercise independent judgment, just as a doctor does when he makes a diagnosis or urges surgery, or a lawyer does when he decides how to handle a case. The key to good journalism is good journalists—educated, thoughtful, caring, probing, and unfettered by prejudice or preconceptions of how the world is.

Television news is not a mirror held up to the world. Reporters, producers, and editors select what will be reported, how much of it will be reported, and in what form. Added to their responsibility for gathering information and shaping it into a news story is the need to make it work in terms of the visual requirements of the medium.

A common problem you may face is that of the news source who is willing to talk, but not on camera. While it is preferable to have videotape of the source, the appropriate attitude is to accept the information in whatever form it is made available. Record the information in your notepad and be prepared to tell what you have learned. The camera operator can find a number of general pictures to serve the voice-over—a sign on the source's desk, the front of his office or building, the news subject himself walking away. Indicate that the source would not talk for the camera, but proceed to quote him as the cover shots are seen. If the source is a well-known public figure, you may be able to obtain a still photo of him, and you can report his words while the photo appears on the screen. An alternative is to tell what the source said in a stand-up from the scene, or working live on camera in the studio. The point to remember is that while it is preferable to have information on videotape, where that is not possible, the information should be included in the story by some other means.

Suppose that an individual refuses to talk with you at all. You can get shots of him walking away, ducking into his car, or slamming the door in your face. Over those pictures, you simply report that the subject had no comment. At least the pictures will show that you attempted to obtain his side of the story. However, do not use this technique simply as a means to embarrass or humiliate individuals who do not want to be interviewed. Exercise restraint and respect the news source's right to privacy and dignity.

Man-in-the-street interviews have their critics as well as their advocates. A man-in-the-street interview is a random, on-camera sampling of public opinion. Reporters can go wrong in the use of this technique when they leave the impression that the sampling has a validity beyond its randomness. When you stand on a street corner and interview the first ten people who come along, and then proceed to extrapolate from that sampling the viewpoints of citizens everywhere, plainly yours is not a careful scientific experiment. It would be wrong to pretend that it is.

However, suppose that you have obtained a report of a respected poll of citizen opinion on a specific issue, and you want to translate that news story into the television medium. You can satisfactorily report the results of the poll, and then use your videotaped sampling of opinion to illustrate the human reality of the information. Furthermore, a random man-in-the-street poll on a lighthearted subject, followed by a disclaimer about its scientific validity and wrapped up with a whimsical close can add a cheerful human touch to an otherwise flagging news program. The important thing is not to leave the impression that the streetcorner people represent anything more than their own individual, untabulated opinions.

Whether he works in print, radio or in television, a reporter has a certain way of looking at the world, and his approach to his work is shaped in part by his perception of the role he plays in society. In his relations with the public, he believes he serves the people's need and right to know what is going on. This is the high-minded side of journalism, the touchstone of the reporter's idealism.

There is, however, another side, the day-by-day operational side—a tough, often cantankerous world where the journalist competes with others both inside and outside his own news organization. Reporters have been known to build reputations on being the fastest, meanest, pushiest kid on the block. Sometimes this aggressive form of journalism is necessary and even laudable; the world is tough and mean in some spots.

However this approach to journalism can get out of hand. If not judiciously tamed, it can lead the reporter to develop a taste for blood. The reporter becomes the hunter in pursuit of the hunted, and everything and everyone are fair game. He loses sight of what serves the public interest and he begins to serve his own interest. He builds up his ego. He enjoys the power. He relishes the thrill of the game. Lost in this process is his capacity to understand and transmit the subtle, even poignant complexity of ideas and events.

A good reporter is like a good detective. He is not content with surface appearances. Rather, he is likely to take note of small details, to ask offbeat and imaginative questions, and to pursue a promising clue with intuition, logic, and tenacity.

However, unlike the detective, the reporter is only rarely investigating a crime. Not everyone in power, not every news source is a crook, although admittedly some few are. To approach the news in the expectation of finding crooks is to warp reality at the outset.

In fact, most of what is reportable lies more in the area of gray than black or white. The reporter has to be as sensitive to impropriety and short-sightedness and human frailty as he is to illegality and malfeasance. And when gathering information as well as reporting it, he needs to exercise consideration and restraint in his manner and delivery.

Reporters often claim that theirs is an adversarial relationship with government officials. However there is a difference between the role of adversary and the role of prosecutor. Although there are some operational principles that lawyers and reporters share, like the careful gathering of evidence and the logical presentation of facts, it is not the job of the reporter to take sides, but rather to lay out the story in an orderly and telling manner, and let the public decide.

Accusatory journalism is jarring. It weakens the case for whatever side the reporter is taking because it insults the intelligence of the reader, listener, or viewer. It intimates that the news consumer is not bright enough to get the point or weigh the evidence on his own.

If this kind of reporting fails miserably in print, it becomes even more unappetizing in the television medium. For example, witness a scene in New York City, where the Mayor is visiting the city's heating complaints office during a brutal cold wave. The telephones are ringing incessantly. Tenants who are trapped in heatless apartments are demanding that the Mayor send help. His Honor talks to the callers, offering sympathy, promising assistance. A television reporter pushes a microphone in front of the Mayor, and asks with a sneer, "Mayor Koch, aren't you just grandstanding here?" To which the Mayor replies with some irritation, "Everytime a Mayor shows he cares, you accuse him of grandstanding!" The result of that interchange was a spitting match between reporter and Mayor, and not much enlightenment for the viewer or explanation or help for the freezing tenants.

Large egos are not unknown among print journalists, but television can seduce even the most principled and self-deprecatory of reporters. There is more show-biz, more hustle in television news, and less time for reflection and the restraining power of second thoughts. The television reporter who comes to see himself first as a personality or a star and only secondarily as a journalist, faces a serious internal conflict, and it may in the end lead him to do strange and terrible things on the air.

On the other hand, there are some reporters in print and broadcasting who just want to win popularity contests. These are the ones who cosy up to the rich, the famous, and the powerful. As it is with the reporter who poses as a brass-knuckled prosecutor, this kind of reporter is likely to be more interested in the world's perceptions of himself than in what the public has the right and need to know. The reporter who needs to be admired and loved, especially by those in power or those who are celebrities, cannot effectively serve either the profession or the public. Dispassion and objectivity become subordinate to the desire for affection and approbation. Even if the reporter should catch the celebrity with his hand in the proverbial cookie jar, he is unlikely to report it, because the reporter now sees himself as a confidant and friend rather than a journalist-observer.

There are numerous potential seductions in the relationship of a newsperson to a news source. Flattery is one of them. For example, artful and cunning mayors know that there is nothing more calculated to win a reporter over to their side than addressing the reporter by name during a televised news conference. "Miss Smith," or better still, "Robyn," thereby becomes a local celebrity, a gratifying development that her boss is sure to notice. However the trap that is thus so cleverly set is this one: After such public recognition, how can Robyn Smith report on the mayor's policy failures or worse without appearing to be an ingrate?

There are more subtle forms of flattery of which a reporter should be aware. Politicians are particularly adept at offering praise for a story, admiring the style of a news report, a hairdo, a suit, or a dress. "How wonderful," you think. "The great man noticed me. He admires me. I must be important." The flattery creates an obstacle for you because you will find it difficult to be hard-nosed or skeptical about someone who has expressed such open admiration for your talents.

In addition to developing appropriate attitudes of mind toward the people you will be covering, it is important to develop a professional attitude toward your work. First, don't worry about bruises on your ego if a producer or an editor suggests that you change a story or approach it in a different way. It is important to develop the capacity to accept honest criticism of your work, and to separate your person, your ego, from the work that you do.

Writing and broadcasting are very personal expressions of one's self. You have to step back from the work, to let it go, and then be prepared to expose it to criticism of the toughest kind. You have to learn to do that, without allowing the criticism to damage your essential perceptions of yourself and your self-worth.

Every reporter, print or broadcast, needs an editor—someone who can second-guess his judgments, someone who can observe his work with fresh, even innocent, eyes. In television news, reporters tend to have more latitude and freedom in shaping the final product than do reporters for newspapers and magazines. The pressures of time, the fact that much of the story has already been committed to videotape before the reporter returns to the station, the limited number of supervisory editorial personnel, and the increasing emphasis on live reporting, all add up to a situation in which what the reporter has to say is likely to go on the air virtually unscrutinized. This may account for some of the idiocies and goofs that sometimes make their way onto the local TV news program. It is a danger that should act as a warning to the self-respecting reporter to develop inner mechanisms for checking personal excesses.

Dignity and credibility in journalism are important values no matter what the medium. However, in television news, where the reporter's face and body appear on the screen along with the story itself, they are easily damaged assets.

To be credible, be consistently accurate. Check your facts. Verify your quotes. Avoid simplifications that can destroy the integrity of meanings.

To be credible, be fair. To some news sources, words are cheap and charges come easy. If you merely transmit those charges and words, without examining the motives and reliability of the source, you can unfairly injure an innocent person. There is much power in being a reporter. Along with that power comes responsibility. Remember that you can damage a life with one thoughtless or careless line, so exercise your power with care.

To be credible, your story has to be balanced. There are two sides to any question. Often there are more than two sides. You owe it to your viewer to offer as much information as you can on all sides of the issue. You have to remain impartial, even when you are transmitting opinions and information with which you personally disagree. You cannot use journalism as a weapon to sell your private causes. There are times when you will have to tell the public about matters that distress you and ideas that go against your personal beliefs. Never withhold information that contradicts your personal beliefs. Tell it straight, tell it fair, and give all sides a chance to be heard.

If, in order to meet these high goals, you find you are going to need more air time for your story, you may have to enter into some hard negotiations with your producer or editor. One argument that you might use is that, after all, television journalism is journalism, and it is inappropriate to trade the values of accuracy, fairness, and balance for the less-admirable values of brevity and sparkle.

CHAPTER NINE.

Evaluating Information

It is not enough for a reporter to gather whatever information he can in the time allowed. He has to make sure that the information he has gathered reflects reality, that it is as true as it is humanly possible to ascertain. This is the process we call evaluating information, and it is one of the most important and challenging aspects of the reporter's work.

The first thing that you have to do is *consider the source*. If the story you are covering is a news event set up by a political figure or the spokesman for a group, then you have to weigh the information you obtain against the *vested interest* of the speaker. A vested interest does not automatically indicate that the information is incorrect or skewed. What it does mean is that you must be alert to the possibility that your information may be only partial and that the source is likely to be casting the information in the best possible light.

Therefore, if the Mayor makes an announcement praising his own achievements, it is entirely appropriate for you to expect the mayor to substantiate his statements with solid evidence. People in high office are constantly bewailing the fact that reporters refuse to accept their statements on faith. The reporter's work certainly would be easier if he could believe everything that he is told. Unfortunately, experience has taught most journalists that it is risky to lodge complete trust in the statements of political figures. The history of journalism is littered with sorry tales of overly trusting reporters who were lied to or who were given partial truths and who, without independently verifying the information, then went on to report it.

I repeat, it is quite appropriate for a reporter to ask a public official to give evidence to support his statements. This should be done calmly, with respect, and without belligerence. There is no need to be argumentative or pugnacious. Quietly and firmly the reporter can demand the facts, and where the official seems to be dodging, press him to answer with words like, "I'm sorry, sir, I don't think you have quite answered my question."

Sometimes a news source will offer a tangled explanation, the kind that you know will be difficult to edit for television. You can quite rightly ask the news source to re-state his position, briefly and plainly. "Can you sum it up in thirty seconds, sir?" is the sort of question that is often necessary in television where the material has to be shaped into a visual and editable form. In fact, this question may even inspire the news source to crystallize his views. Where an earlier response rambled because he was searching for a way to formulate his answer, this time the news source may be more precise and concise. Just as the print reporter looks for a good quote, the television reporter looks for one, but preferably in a form that can be edited for videotape.

A useful technique for testing the validity of a source's statements is to play devil's advocate—to confront the individual with the counterarguments of the other side and ask him to respond. Again, it is important that you ask these questions in a calm manner, making it plain that you are seeking information rather than taking sides.

In addition to considering the quality of the information obtained from the source, evaluate the merits of the source itself. For whom does this person speak? Whom does he represent? Sometimes you will be confronted by an organization with a high-sounding title, and an articulate spokesman, that actually consists of only a handful of members. It is appropriate, even necessary, that the reporter ask the spokesman to substantiate his claim to speak for a certain group of people. Questions like: how many members belong to your organization? will you give me the records to show how many and who belong? how many active members are there? how were you chosen to lead them? what percentage of the group you say you represent actually belongs to the organization? are any contrary views reflected inside the organization?

These questions are particularly valuable if you are covering a neighborhood or groups whose interests are not easily defined. Often it is the most militant segment of the population that organizes and speaks out, while more moderate voices remain silent or untapped. It is imperative that you weigh the validity of statements by self-appointed community leaders who may in fact speak for the few rather than the many. Or, if these voices are to be aired, then place the situation in context, and try to balance the story with countervailing viewpoints.

It is enormously seductive to turn to the most visually arresting and colorful personality as spokesman for a group, but it is oversimplistic where the choice does not reflect truth, and it is also poor journalism.

This is not to argue that reporters should refuse to make an effort to find out what ordinary citizens think and feel. It is merely to indicate how difficult it can be to find out which opinions are valid, representative, and carry weight. Some practical definition of "a leader" is necessary, and perhaps the most honest way to deal with the matter is to state plainly in the news story how many the leader actually speaks for rather than how many he claims to represent. The reality instead of the appearance is what should be reported.

It is because it is so hard to determine whose voice speaks for the ordinary citizen that many reporters turn readily and with relief to officially designated spokesmen. The public information officer or the corporate public relations officer—affectionately called "flaks"—represent definable groups and organizations. They often have at their disposal resources for printing background material and for providing sophisticated services for television as well as print reporters. They oil the wheels of intercourse between the press and government or the press and large organizations, and many reporters welcome the clean simplicity of this arrangement. Cloaked with the authority of the organization that he or she represents, the spokesperson can issue statements which you can accept as reliable.

Or can you?

Suppose that the spokesman is the public relations or information officer of a large corporation. Is he telling you all there is to know, or just what he was told to tell? And how well-informed is he? It is appropriate for you to ask such a spokesman to state the source of *his* information, to explain whether in fact he obtained his information directly from the chairman of the board or the president of the corporation, and whether he was privy to the inside process of decision-making.

It is common practice for a top official in government or business to avoid direct contact with his press spokesman, in order to maintain his "deniability." That is, should it be later revealed that the spokesman misinformed the press, the top man can deny responsibility because he did not speak directly with the spokesman. It is a neat trick. Government leaders do it. So do corporate chiefs, Cabinet secretaries, heads of foundations, universities, and unions. For a reporter, these practices make it harder to unearth the truth. For the public, they make it difficult to know what words are worth believing and what words are balderdash. This is one reason why a good reporter will try to talk with the man at the top of the organization, and will feel uncomfortable with information gleaned only from spokesmen and information officers.

Furthermore, the single voice assigned to speak for a large agency or organization gives the appearance of a monolithic opinion, which in most cases is not the reality. Certainly, you should obtain this official view, and challenge it where and when you think it appropriate; but you should not be satisfied that this process alone will give you a semblance of truth. Try to cross-check the information with other people inside the organization, search for evidence of a contrary opinion, and try to discover the nature of the internal debates that took place before the official position was reached. In sum, the reporter has to give the public more than unvarnished official voices. The purpose of good journalism is to explain, shed light, and give insight.

It is plain from all of this that you have to be on your guard, that you have to regularly consider what to believe and what not to believe. It is a psychological fact that people prefer to believe what they want to believe and will shut out information that contradicts their strongly held beliefs. This being so, you must be doubly careful that you are not turning off information you neither wanted nor expected to receive.

The reporter has to be on guard against personal prejudices. If she is middle-class, is she more inclined to trust a spokesman who uses middle-class English, dresses in a middle-class suit, and thus makes her feel comfortable? If he is black, is he more inclined to believe a black source than a white one, because he feels an affinity for the speaker? The reporter has to separate his private-citizen opinions from what ought to be an impartial, professional way of viewing people, events, and information.

Being human, the unwary reporter may be hornswoggled by appearances. One of the biggest traps is the "charm factor." The reporter comes to like a particular news figure and that colors the way he views what the news figure is saying and doing. Or conversely, the reporter takes a personal dislike to someone in the news, and that, too, colors the way that he reports on that individual's activities.

The reporter may feel a stronger sympathy for underdogs than for those who have wealth and power. Thus, she may be inclined to favor the complaints of the tenant, and discount the explanations of the landlord, even when the complete story, if unearthed, would reveal fault enough on both sides. The reporter who sees herself as a crusader or an advocate for one side of a case is likely to be led astray from the truth, and in the end serve neither those she is defending nor the public.

The appropriate mindset for the reporter is that truth must be pursued fairly and evenhandedly, and let the chips fall where they may. It may feel good to ask tough questions of the government welfare officer or the landlord. Go right ahead. Ask them. But the same skeptical, probing approach must be applied to the clients—to the recipients of welfare, to the tenants. This means approaching all people with some skepticism, some sense that statements for the television camera tend to be self-promotional, regardless of the source.

The welfare recipient who is complaining about a raw deal needs to be subjected to the same professional probing as the chief of the welfare department. The surprising thing is that, the deeper you probe, the more evenhanded you are in your interviews and research, the more complex the issues appear to be.

For example: A television reporter aired a story about a group of people who were living in cardboard boxes in the shadow of the Capitol dome in Washington, D.C. The people complained that they had been rendered homeless when the city boarded up the crumbling houses where they had been living, with the intent to tear them down. They argued that nobody was doing anything for them, and they blamed their situation on the cold, heartless, and unfeeling officials of the city. It was a powerful and dramatic human story, and once it was aired, city authorities stepped forward to offer prompt assistance. It seemed at that juncture that the television news story had achieved some social good.

However, a few days later, the reporter decided to do a follow-up story. She was startled to find that these same people were still living in their cardboard boxes. They had spurned all offers of help, preferring instead the freedom and rent-free advantages of their makeshift cardboard housing. The moral of that story, as it was subsequently told by the reporter, is that human beings can be contrary, and that sometimes people would rather go their own way than accept help.

For the reporter whose natural instinct is to explain all human problems in sociological terms, that kind of truth is both educational and enlightening. There are in fact occasions when people turn out to be responsible for their own predicaments.

Good reporting does not merely say, "this is the situation, and tut-tut, isn't it terrible!" Good reporting attempts to come to grips with the "why" of things. Much local reporting fails because there is little effort to explain and to place events and issues in broad context.

For example, here is a typical story in a big city like New York: It is winter, and in tenements around the city, pipes are freezing in buildings where inadequate heat is being provided. In some buildings, there is no heat at all. The television reporter interviews the old woman who is sitting propped up in bed, covered with coats and blankets. She is trying to heat her apartment with the flame from her gas stove in the kitchen. The story shows the shivering woman, her valiant efforts to stay warm, the icicles in the bathroom, the grim, ugly picture of human denial and suffering. The building superintendent says the boiler is broken, and he doesn't know when it will be repaired. The camera operator moves to the basement and there the camera roams over the ancient black boiler, which appears to have died of old age. In his closing stand-up the reporter says that he has been trying to reach the landlord or the agents for the building, but they refused to answer his calls. Over and out.

The impression left with the viewer is that the landlord is a wicked monster who likes to freeze old ladies while he piles up a small fortune in rents. All of the latter may in fact be true, but the reporter has failed to prove it. However, this kind of reporting offers a simple means of dealing with reality—the good guys versus the bad guys; and the landlord must be the bad guy because he is the fellow who owns the building. Right?

Well, maybe. However, it is likely that the real story is far more complicated. Some digging into the tax records and profits of the landlord, plus telephoned questions directed at city housing authorities and landlord representatives, could lend greater depth and insight. Instead of the obvious and banal story of the shivering tenant and the "wicked" landlord, the reporter might come up with the more edifying story of how rent control and inflation, combined with the presence of tenants who fail to pay their rent and who cannot be evicted under city law, are making it difficult for some landlords to keep their buildings in repair. That is not as sexy a story as the wicked landlord, of course, and it fails to solve the immediate problem of the freezing tenant; but it does provide information that sheds light on the situation. A useful follow-up story would then be based on questions like: how can this problem be solved? who is working on possible solutions? and who should be responsible for balancing the rights and needs of those involved? These basic questions, directed at the Mayor, or the urban affairs divisions of the city's universities, could develop into a fine, thoughtful piece of television journalism.

Plainly one of the keys to obtaining useful information, and evaluating it intelligently, is asking the right questions. The right questions are neither the obvious nor the banal or surface questions. Much of the news is not a matter of good-versus-bad, but rather a matter of rights in conflict. Television no less than print can deal with these matters if you resist the temptation to oversimplify where the reality is in fact complex.

Simplification is of course one of the techniques used by all journalists when reporting the news. You must act as the bridge between a complex reality and the citizen unschooled in the particular background, substance, and techniques necessary to unravel that reality. You have the often difficult job of ascertaining which among the many available facts are important, and which are irrelevant. You have to take those facts and present them in ways that will be easily understood—and at the same time make sure that other facts, opinions, and viewpoints are heard. Then, too, you must avoid simplifying an issue to the point where you present only *two* sides, when in fact there are *several*. The aim is to simplify, but not *over*-simplify, a difference that will be clarified for the new reporter over time and with careful attention to the principles of fairness and balance. While this is a problem faced by all reporters, the burden is made greater by the brevity of the TV news product.

The problem of authenticating information can be troublesome when reporting disaster stories. You would expect an eyewitness account of a disaster to be reliable, but that is often not the case. Ordinary citizens can be terrible witnesses. They can imagine things or hype them or pretend that they saw something they did not see, just to get themselves on television. Do not, under any circumstances, underestimate the latter motivation. For some people, to appear on television is to come alive, to grow large, to become important. Having been near a disaster, they will make up, embroider, even lie once the camera is pointed in their direction.

To some extent, you can protect yourself from these artful fabricators by doing a little checking before videotaping the interview. Ask the "witness" where he was standing when it all happened, ask him to describe things in detail rather than vague generalities, and always look for precision in the description. The question, "What was the first thing that you heard or saw?" followed by "And what happened next," and "What exactly did you see," can help a great deal. In the end, there is no better way to cover yourself than to round up a number of eyewitnesses, if they are available, and to show the public the contradictions if they exist. The cross-checking of evidence is a vital part of journalism.

Television reporters, particularly local reporters, tend to shy away from complex, statistical stories because they are hard to shape into visual material. This constitutes a form of criminal neglect because so much important news is based on reports and statistical compilations. It also leaves the reporter open to being manipulated by news sources who use the statistics to say what they want the numbers to say.

However, on behalf of the thoughtful citizen, the reporter could be asking: what do these charts actually measure? Do the statistics focus on the right questions or do they merely measure what it is traditional to measure? Do they measure what is easy to measure, excluding verities that are important for public understanding?

For example, in these times when even economists are openly questioning traditional economic theories, it is quite appropriate for a reporter to ask whether the Gross National Product (GNP) measures all the productivity of the people, including unpaid bartered labor, self-help, and so forth. It is appropriate to ask whether output per worker should be measured by the hour or by the output per dollar of wages paid. The reporter ought to know the difference between a statistical average and a mean, and be aware of how the results of a report can be slanted according to which form is chosen. Statistics can lie, do lie, and will lie, so long as reporters gobble them whole and fail to evaluate the information carefully.

Turning complex reports, charts, and statistics into television news stories requires considerable skill on many fronts. You must thoroughly understand the material at hand if you are to determine which are the highlights and most significant passages you want to quote. You will then work with the graphics division at your station to design a story that will be interesting visually and at the same time explain its contents clearly and effectively.

Printed matter culled out of the report can either appear in still flashes, or it can be rolled on the screen while you read the material. The quality of the writing for this kind of complex story is important: it must be especially clear, precise, and well-reasoned. To turn ostensibly dry and dull statistical material into living, significant television is a high art, but one that is well worth developing. Since so many members of the public now turn to television as their chief source of news, it is important that news be defined as information the public needs to know, even if it is hard to translate these particular stories into the visual medium.

Obviously, no general assignment reporter can be an expert in every field. It is therefore important that you build up a collection of contacts you can tap on short notice to help explain complex material. The expert source may be another reporter who has substantive expertise. He may be someone inside a public interest group, although public interest groups can at times slant information just as some members of establishment institutions do. You will need to apply critical judgment to the individuals you use to explain complex material, but once a trusted contact is developed, you can feel secure about seeking that individual's help.

On numerous occasions, you will have to enlist expert opinion. But which experts? And how do you define an expert? Whether in the field of science, psychology, economics, politics, or education, one man's expert can be another man's charlatan. A certain individual may have been quoted for years as an expert, and as a result he now carries the image of authority. However neither his credentials nor his wisdom have been subjected to recent and close scrutiny. Nor has an effort been made to discover *other* individuals who may be more knowledgeable and quotable than he.

Newspaper clippings have a way of creating experts simply by virtue of the term being appended to a name once or twice. Television reporters who are plunged into a new subject will grasp at the printed name, feeling that it is safe to quote that person as an expert because after all the local paper says it is so. It is possible, however, that this anointed guru gained his early prominence simply because he had friends at the newspaper or was clever at self-promotion. Sometimes, in this casual fashion, a certain point of view, a specific expertness, becomes the one that is cited repeatedly, and in that way excludes from public view a variety of alternative expertness.

It is natural for the citizen in a complex world to prefer his information to arrive in simple and reliable forms, and reporters do try to give the public what it wants. One part of the reporter's job is to create order and find meaning in events and issues that are confused and chaotic. There he is, Charlie Candor, with his honest face and his authoritative voice, telling the public how it is. Out of all the possible material to choose from he has plucked these tidbits and shaped them into a whole story. And then—here is the expert, silver-haired Dr. Dogma, spouting his certainties. Why should the reporter go beyond what the expert says when what he says is so comforting and so well said?

Why indeed? Because more often than not, experts will and do disagree. Their truth is no more holy and perfect than anybody else's and reporters do the public a disservice if they pretend otherwise. The purpose of news is not to offer pablum simplicities, but rather to inform the people in as complete and truthful a fashion as possible. The careful reporter will not settle for the quick, the easy, and the obvious, but will seek out a number of voices and viewpoints because reality is rarely so neat and simple as the single expert says it is. What do you do when experts disagree? You air the disagreements, weigh them, and then let the public be the judge.

Finally, evaluating information requires that you be aware of the developing patterns in information. Two and two appear to make four, but is that really all there is? For example, when you are covering the political scene, one or two politicians may be disagreeing substantively with their Party leader. Are these one or two mavericks, or are their positions early signs of a general mutiny or shift? Do you report only that two political figures are saying things that differ from the official party line, or do you dig for possible evidence that this may be the surfacing of a deeper pattern of change? Which is better journalism—that two and two make four, or that two and two could indicate a development of larger significance, a crack in the Party's hegemony?

Although television news reporting requires much of its reporters in terms of controlling the visual data, directing the camera crews, and packaging stories, television reporters are not relieved of their responsibility for the higher forms of journalism. Context, meaning, insight can be conveyed by a reporter who cares enough and who refuses to be satisfied with the obvious and the surface realities of any story.

CHAPTER TEN.

How To Cover a Speech, News Conference, or Hearing

Speeches, news conferences, and hearings are staples of the newsperson's diet. These are planned news events, some more newsworthy than others. A few basic procedures can help to free you from the routine aspects of the assignment so that you can concentrate on evaluating information and shaping the video package.

In most cases, the speech or the testimony is available in advance. A quick telephone call to the press officer of the public figure can determine when the material will be available. Usually, you can pick up the printed speech or testimony on the scene, before the proceedings begin. Arrive well before the start of the event, so you can read through the speech or testimony in advance.

You will be reading with two purposes. First, the substance of the matter. What is the focus of the speech? Is it new and newsworthy? Is it substantive? Has it wider significance? If the answer is yes, read the speech again. This time, you are looking for specific nuggets that best illustrate or clarify the point the speaker intends to make. You then mark up these passages clearly on the copy. You can judge the length of these potential sound-bites by their printed length, and thus decide in advance the sections of the speech you want your camera to capture. As the speaker approaches that particular illustrative section, give your cameraperson ample warning so that he can shoot the last phrases of the previous sentence and then shoot the specific part that you want. Allow him to shoot several phrases beyond the section you intend to use. This procedure will ensure that the camera is up to speed before the significant sound-bite is captured, and shooting beyond the end of the speech will help in the editing later.

Use specific signals for your cameraperson in these circumstances. If you remain standing next to the camera, a gentle tap on the cameraman's shoulder will signal start and stop. If you sit in the audience, raise your hand, snap your fingers, or just turn around and nod to the cameraperson.

The object is to cover yourself in terms of reporting the speech by having on videotape the segments that seem most promising. If nothing better eventuates during the question and answer period, then at least the basic story is in hand.

Another advantage to planning the sections that you want to shoot is that you can then free the cameraperson to take cutaway shots during those times when he does not have to be rolling on the speech. The camera can be removed from its fixed position on the tripod and then go portable. The cutaways normally include videotape of members of the audience listening, pictures shot from behind the speaker and toward the spectators, pictures of the station's reporter listening or taking notes, and shots of other cameras in action.

There is at least one possible trap in all of this. Sometimes the printed speech serves only as a jumping-off point for the speaker. He may decide to digress in significant ways. If that is so, often the digressions are of more interest than the planned address. A warning here: avoid the temptation to be inattentive simply because you have pulled some quotes from the speech. Read along with the speaker to make sure that he does in fact say what he planned to say, and where he appears to be throwing away his scripted speech, listen carefully and ask the camera operator to capture this material. Significant digressions should be marked on the pre-speech version of the copy.

There are times when a speaker will decide to cut his speech short and he will instead refer reporters to his printed copy. If the significant passages you were seeking are in the printed material but were not spoken on camera, they can be referred to in your voice-over, or you can try to obtain them in a different form during the q and a afterward.

Suppose that the speaker has important things to say, but says them badly. Perhaps, he mumbles, head down, using turgid and obfuscating language. Do you say to yourself "this is a dud story"? Some reporters will give up on the story because the speaker is unexciting. However, if what is being said is important enough, then it is up to you to find a way to tell it that will attract and hold the viewer's attention. If the public has the need and right to know this information, the dullness and turgidity of the speaker should be secondary considerations.

How then do you manage to turn a stone into a sparkler? You wait for the question-and-answer period that normally follows a speech or news conference. (We will deal with public hearings later.) Even as the speaker intones his prepared remarks, you are thinking of ways to obtain the information you want in the form that will be most usable in terms of the medium. You are planning one or two questions for the speaker, preferably strong, provocative questions that will bring a sparkle to his eyes and a humanized response. A warning here: do not ask "yes-or-no" questions because what you are likely to get on tape is a "yes-or-no" answer rather than the full, explanatory statement that you are seeking. The better questions will be based on the prepared text. They will be follow-ups like "why" or "how do you account for" and "how do you explain."

Another technique is to play devil's advocate: "Your opponent [or the opposition] says this and that. How do you answer his charges?" Thus you have the news source no longer with his head buried in his speech and droning on in written prose-style, but instead you have him looking up and out at the audience, his face (hopefully) mobile and reacting. Before you pose your question, make sure that your camera is rolling in order to catch the reaction to the question as you are asking it as well as the subsequent answer. You should also carry either a hand-held microphone or wear a lavalier microphone so that the sound of your question is captured by the camera as well as the speaker's reply.

There is one problem with the above approach. If you elicit a lively response from the speaker, it is not only *your* camera that will catch it. So will all the other cameras from competing stations. In essence, you are doing their work for them. Your competitors will subsequently cut out your question, use the answer, and make it appear that their own inveterate reporter did the work. This probably does not matter much unless you are jealous of your work and prefer to have exclusives.

One solution is to save your best questions for the period when both the speech and the q and a are over. Have your camera crew packed up and ready to move forward to approach the speaker for a one-on-one interview. You can then ask your questions for your camera alone and even follow up without interference. Some speakers have no objection to being approached after a speech. Others do. High officials may have bodyguards around them to fend off reporters. You should do the best that you can to persuade the speaker to grant you a few moments, but avoid being pushy or surly if you are refused.

In sum, be alert to possibilities for the story and do not give up, no matter how unpromising the original proceedings. If the whole event is awful although its newsworthiness remains, you may want to take your camera crew to the scene of the material under discussion—a housing development, if the subject is public housing, police station, if it is crime, and so forth. In other words, show with pictures what the speaker is talking about, using the information in the speech or news conference as a jumping off point for the visual story. You should try, too, to obtain an interview with people of contrasting opinions, if the story lends itself to that concept. Before or during the speech, you can telephone your news desk and ask your editor to set up a relevant interview for you to do following the speech or news conference.

However, at times all you plan to include in your story is the event itself. If you intend to tape your stand-up at the event you should be writing it during the speech. Practiced reporters will tape their stand-ups on the scene either as the event is unfolding or as it is breaking up. This lends drama to the report by showing the reporter at the scene interpreting the event before the viewer's eyes. If you do your stand-up while the conference or speech is going on, avoid interfering with or interrupting the event. Stand at the back of the room with your back to the podium and speak in a low voice directly into the microphone. Sometimes an on-the-scene stand-up becomes necessary because of the press of time. A deadline may be approaching, or the camera crew is to be reassigned to another story. It is always a good idea to begin working on the script for your stand-up as early as possible, just in case your assignment desk has to call the crew (or you) away to another story. In this way you have on videotape the nearly complete components of your story.

Suppose that there is a speech or a news conference and a number of spectators disrupt the proceedings? Suppose that they erupt in anger, shout questions, and try to rattle the official speaker? In short, suppose that you have a fine old donnybrook on your hands? Can you resist making the disruption the center of your story?

You should be aware that this kind of manipulation by counter-forces is a growing practice among some people who have learned how to play on television's proclivity for the dramatic. The protestors want to distract attention away from the speaker and thus to render him silent. Since they are unable to remove his First Amendment right to speak freely, they will try to shout him down and disrupt the meeting. They use every means to lure the camera in their direction, and away from the podium.

It may be that the complaints of the disrupters are valid, and the protest is just a means to publicly air their grievances. The reporter must weigh all these possibilities to make sure that he is not being used either by the official speaker or by the dissidents in the audience. How to handle the story?

It only takes one or two noisy people to disrupt a meeting. But even if several dozen are disrupting, ask yourself do they represent a wider population or are they merely noisy dissidents who enjoy creating a fuss? Is the outrage real or concocted? Is it valid, based on individual complaints, or a rage against the universe? These are tough questions to answer, but do attempt to answer them. Upon these answers will depend the final story.

For example, if you choose one way, the anchor lead-in to your story will be that the Mayor spoke to a group of citizens and he said this and that. The Mayor will say his piece on videotape and then there will be a small clip of the audience disturbance, followed by a return to the central issues raised by his honor. The disruption will be mentioned, but relegated to a minor place in the story.

If you think the protesters have a real case, then, after the meeting, you should do some interviews with them, on camera, to give them the opportunity to support and validate their case and to argue it against your probing questions. The kind of questions you might ask are these: "What precisely is your complaint against the Mayor?" and "What exactly do you expect him to do?" In other words, you will be attempting to shed light on the issues that divide the citizens from the Mayor instead of airing a pointless heated exchange that explains nothing except that certain people are angry and they have brought their anger to a public forum. If your interviews appear to indicate that the protesters have a case, then the anchor lead-in would be that the Mayor went to the people to tell them about this and that, *but* he was confronted by a group of protesters who wanted him to do something else. The final story would give the Mayor a chance to be heard, but it would lead swiftly to the exchanges inside the hall and then to the later interviews outside where the people explained their specific grievances. A more complete story would require some comment from the Mayor or city hall on those grievances, and an attempt should be made to get that response.

From the above you can see that the reporter is not a passive conduit for information or events. He must make highly skilled and professional judgments and not allow himself to be co-opted by manipulators of any persuasion or by organized spectacles.

There are some news directors or producers who will observe that the competition used lively videotape of the disruptions and will berate the reporter who chooses to opt for something different. Be prepared to defend your decision on the ground of integrity and commitment to old-fashioned principle.

Another staple event for news coverage is the public hearing. As with a speech or a news conference, make sure that you have in hand all the advance material. The prepared testimony of witnesses should be handled in the same fashion as a prepared speech. At a hearing, however, the question-and-answer period is not an exchange between the news figure and the press. Instead it is an exchange between those officials who arranged the hearing, and the witness.

Covering a hearing requires a high degree of attentiveness on the part of the reporter and the camera crew. At any moment a vital exchange can take place, producing the appropriate videotaped nugget that will go to the heart of the story. Don't videotape the entire event. Listen to each question, and where one of them promises a fruitful answer, ask the camera operator to roll. There will be sundry false starts, dull bits where you expected something good to emerge, but there is neither rest nor relief in the effort to pin down this kind of story.

Some early legwork can be of enormous help to you. If you know in advance that you are to be assigned to cover the hearing it is useful to telephone the officials or the appropriate staff of the officials who will be doing the interrogating. Find out from the chairman, for example, what exactly it is that he wants and expects to learn from the witness's testimony, and what questions he is prepared to ask. If you inform yourself about which city councilman or senator or other official is well prepared for the question-and-answer period, you can be forewarned to train your camera on him when he cross-examines. In other words, if you are familiar with the officials on the panel, and you know which of them does his homework or cares a great deal about the subject, or who is likely to substantively challenge the witness, you can then predict that these individuals are likely to produce the most newsworthy exchanges. In anticipation of these exchanges bearing fruit, ask your cameraperson to roll when they begin their questioning.

Keep good notes during the hearing, writing down significant material that was not videotaped. This material can be useful for the stand-up. From out of it the reporter may draw a telling phrase, or an apt quote that sums up the meaning of the event or places it in perspective.

As in any other journalism assignment, ask key questions—if not verbally in an exchange with a news figure, then in your head. Of a hearing, you might ask: Why was the hearing called? What did the committee hope to achieve by it? What events led up to it? Why was this particular witness called? How valid is the case that he made? Was the questioning pointed and substantive, or were the members of the committee posturing for political purposes? Did the committee members do their homework and were they trying to get at the facts or was this just an effort to placate public opinion?

The answers to these and other questions will help to determine the final story. The anchor lead-in written by the reporter will either be a funnel for a "today-this-happened" story, implying that this was a hearing worthy of serious consideration and useful to the public; or else it may be an anchor lead-in that places the hearing in a different perspective, showing it to be more political circus than an attempt to design legislation or change a situation. Again, apply a skeptical, professional intelligence to the event and the material before you. There is no pure objectivity in reporting, because plainly the fact of deciding a lead, deciding what to put in and what to leave out, means that you are injecting yourself into the coverage. But that self should be professional, impartial, unbiased and fair.

Finally, there may be times when you will want to question the witness before your camera. This will require a stake-out in the hallway after the event, or during a lunch break. In a stake-out, you move your camera to the door outside of the hearing room, and catch the witness as he is leaving, or invite him to be questioned before your stationary camera. You should have prepared a few good, probing questions to ask and move quickly to the heart of the subject. Often a witness will not be happy about the interview situation, and he will walk away after the first question or two. So move in fast and dispense with the preliminary small-talk.

As was said earlier, speeches, news conferences, and hearings are basic components of any news day. On the surface they are unexciting events calculated to inspire less than enthusiastic attention by reporters who prefer more interesting visual assignments. Yet these events often involve the meat-and-potatoes of news—that is, issues that are significant and highly news-worthy. When handled by a television reporter with intelligence, probity, and skill, they can provide information of singular importance and genuine utility to the viewing public.

CHAPTER ELEVEN.

Covering a Demonstration

Television commercials instruct us in a common wisdom: that one spray with a particular deodorant or daily brush with a certain toothpaste will bring love and eternal peace of mind. We watch the commercials knowing that these promises are nonsense, but we buy just the same.

In most entertainment programs the message is hardly more subtle. When faced with a serious problem, we are told, the solutions are easily discernible and readily available within an hour or a half-hour span of time: one can resort to divorce, murder, antic comedy, or a shootout at the OK Corral.

Television is an imperfect instrument for projecting the patient, tiresome, agonizing negotiation necessary to manage the real problems that face real people. As a dramatic medium, television strips reality of the routine and the dull, and presents a picture of ready success or instant denouement where life is often marred by uncertainty or failure.

In a story written by Edwin Keister Jr., in *TV Guide* on August 14, 1982, Sgt. George McCormick, a Los Angeles police officer, compared his real-life work with that of a typical cops-and-robbers show on television: "You guys can cram more police work into an hour than I do in a year," he said. . . . "People say, 'Why can't the real police be like that?' They don't understand that someone's writing a script and there's always action and it'll turn out right."

McCormick went on. "Some days I go all day without a call. Other days it's call, call, call. One of my ex-partners defined police work best: 'Hours of boredom punctuated by minutes of sheer terror.' "

Television's shortcomings in terms of reflecting reality are not confined to commercials and dramas alone. They also infect television news, where the public expectation of reality is greater. The demand for visual drama and for brevity limits the capacity of television news to explain the complexity of certain issues or to deal with them in depth. Longer programs do not necessarily lead to greater depth. In local stations, where more program time is available now than ever before, the tendency is to use the extra time for more stories and more entertainment rather than for longer explanatory and background pieces.

It is ironic that at a time when social, economic, and political problems are growing more complex and more difficult to solve, increasing numbers of citizens are turning for their information to a medium that tends to deal in simplistic images. In the non-television reality, even if the rights and wrongs of things can be identified, the how-to-act-upon-them is muddled and difficult. We face rights in conflict and the consequent need to make agonizing tradeoffs. In its brief and epigrammatic way television tends to define complex and multi-faceted issues as struggles between the good guys and the bad guys, and thus helps create a climate in which the citizen viewer may be unwilling to either recognize or accept the compromises necessary for civil equity and peace.

The persistent use of the demonstration as a public forum for complex issues, and television's fascination with these events as both drama and entertainment, illustrate this point. An organized demonstration is a staged event, just as a news conference is a staged event. Both are designed to attract the attention of the news media.

The attraction of demonstrations is obvious. They are visually interesting. Masses of people raising their fists, shouting, and chanting create drama and color. There is emotion. The demonstration offers to angry and frustrated people a public release for their pent-up feelings. Furthermore, demonstrations simplify issues while they offer producers relief from talking heads in councils and hearing rooms.

That demonstrations are attractive to news organizations is not lost on those who plan them. Organizers will make certain that the local TV stations know where and at what time the event is scheduled to take place. The demonstration does not have to be serious or represent a broad spectrum of opinion to attract coverage. As long as it is lively, theatrical, and visually interesting, the demonstrators can almost certainly count on the cameras to be there.

Many demonstrations are organized simply because that is the only way that its supporters can win the attention of the news media. Without a reporter, producer, or editor on the staff of the station to argue for them and for their issue, they know that they have little chance of attracting the interest of the news organization.

Even where it is acknowledged that the complexity of the issues that divide them from their government or from other citizens might best be explained in quiet and thoughtful interviews, the organizers turn instead to demonstrations as the only perceived means to be heard. They resort to an emotional and confrontational form of free speech where perhaps some earlier, thoughtful attention on the part of reporters would have made possible temperate, rational, and constructive dialogue.

As a result, everybody is doing it: the elderly, the handicapped, Puerto Rican nationalists, Croatians, anti-nuclear-war protesters, Jane Fonda, farmers, welfare mothers, construction workers, the unemployed, tenants . . . the list is endless; and as the cacophony rises and their numbers increase, demonstrations tend to lose their effectiveness in either arousing public opinion or shaping official response. To the television viewer, it becomes one more spectacle to be watched with amusement and bemusement, and then forgotten.

Why local television fails to cover certain issues before citizens feel the need to demonstrate is a compound of many factors. The first can be traced to the caliber of reporter that is hired by managements in some small, and large, markets. Where the reporter's appearance, dramatic ability, and wizardry with visual packaging take precedence over his commitment to and understanding of the needs of the local community, that emphasis will be reflected in the final news product. That the reporter has sources in the community, and is trusted and respected there, becomes secondary to his on-air personality and his looks. In many cases, reporters are hired from outside of the station's area, and arrive on the scene lacking the knowledge, insight, or contacts necessary to be effective local enterprise journalists.

Even where the reporter has had time to develop a concern for and contacts with local groups, his length of service at a particular local station is likely to be limited. There is a constant turnover of personnel in local television news. Reporters barely have time to learn the name of the local mayor or how to find their way through the city's streets when they move on to another station in another city in search of higher salaries and a larger viewing audience. Because of this singular lack of continuity, few television reporters remain at a local station long enough to build up the sense of caring, commitment, and trust that community groups need and want.

Even if the reporter is eager to make these contacts, at most local stations he is likely to be kept too busy to pursue the inclination. Local reporters are often required to cover three and four stories every day and as a result they can hardly be expected to do more than dust the surface of the events that pass before them. While the best reporting is not a reaction to events but rather an anticipation of developments, the television reporter who is spared little time for reflection or for the pursuit of enterprise stories has little opportunity to practice such higher-level journalism.

Plainly, the real world of local television—as it is now constituted—is neither an ideal nor a perfect world, and the reporter must make the best of what opportunities he has to practice intelligent journalism.

It is another morning at your station. You are, of course, overworked, and you are now presented with an assignment to cover a demonstration. Your first step is to telephone the organizers before the demonstration begins and find out the purpose of the event. You may also want to talk with whoever represents the opposing viewpoints or positions, so that you have a rounded picture of what is at stake. It is useful to do advance legwork for a demonstration so that you can obtain background information in a quiet, thoughtful setting, away from the noise and hullabaloo of the event that is soon to take place. The nature of the information you obtain will be different—more reflective, more sober—when you get it in a telephone interview or in a quiet setting. In the middle of a demonstration, organizers and participants tend to hype their demands or raise the ante. The presence of the camera and the excitement of the occasion can combine to reshape the nature of the group's demands. Certainly it is important to evaluate the goals of the organizers and to weigh the seriousness and validity of their intentions.

Once you learn what the demonstrators want, you should ask yourself whether the demands are achievable. For example, it comes as no surprise when citizens demonstrate to keep bus and subway fares down. However, for many reasons, the transportation system is in serious deficit. If the riders are unwilling to pay the cost of running the system, who should? What exactly are the demonstrators proposing?

If in fact what is demanded is overly simplistic and eminently not doable, the reporter owes it to the viewer to do more than expose the demonstrators'

anger and frustration. To record the anger and frustration without analysis
and without perspective is to add heat without shedding any light. The reporter is merely saying, "Look, people are mad," but offering no explanation
of how those grievances might be abolished.

Plainly, a simple show-and-tell demonstration story ill-serves the public's
right to know and adds emotion and unreason instead of knowledge to the
public dialogue. If you are to act responsibly, you must inform the viewer
about what is involved in solving this particular problem, what the options
are, where the money might come from, and whether the funds are available. This would in no way silence or ignore the voices of demonstrating
citizens who feel powerless and imposed upon, but it would add to their
outcry a dispassionate explanation of what is at stake.

There are at least two ways to approach the challenge of reporting a demonstration. One is to view it as an event with a meaning and a purpose
beyond the moment, that is, as a goad for investigating the issues that are
thus raised. The other is to view the demonstration simply as street theater,
a passing spectacle with no life or purpose beyond the moment. In most
cases television news tends to cover these events as spectacle and theater.
However, even here you need to apply careful analysis and evaluation, if
you are to keep yourself from being swept along by the visual seductions
orchestrated by the demonstration's leaders.

A key piece of information is how many people there are in the gathering.
Sometimes the demonstration is small enough for you to take your own
count; but usually you are going to have to rely on figures provided by the
police. Police numbers should be attributed to the police, not accepted as
gospel truth. Depending upon the nature of the protest, officials have been
known to undercount or overcount. If the demonstrators constitute a group
that officials view with distaste, their numbers can be projected at a low
figure to give the impression that the demonstration is not very serious. On
the other hand, leaders of the demonstration may provide inflated figures in
order to make the protest appear more significant. If you approach the event
aware of how the figures can be manipulated, you can then report honestly
that the crowd *estimates* range from one figure to another, and leave it to
the viewer to draw his own conclusion.

Another question that needs to be answered is, what is the nature of the
crowd? How many participants are true demonstrators and how many have
merely been drawn to the scene by the spectacle and the excitement? A

random sampling can be of help to you, although firm figures will be nearly impossible to pin down. Interviewing participants with the cameras off is a valuable technique. A simple interview, without videotape, is less likely to lead to manipulation by ordinary citizens, some of whom will create lively fictions to ensure their appearance on television.

The reporter has to separate those who are willing to say *anything* for the cameras from those who have something significant and legitimate to say. Some television reporters will accept a demonstrator's on-camera comments uncritically because in effect the comments serve the reporter's plans for a dramatic news package. That gutsy, pithy, startling statement makes a good story, so why bother to challenge or ignore it? The result is the skewing of reality, the perversion of truth, in a flimflamming contretemps between the citizen and the reporter. The newsgathering process becomes more of a conspiracy to create drama than a reflection of sober journalistic truths.

A demonstration consists of a crowd which has a life and purpose of its own, an entity which in a way is separate from the individuals within the crowd who may or may not feel an identity with the movement that surrounds them. As soon as possible, identify not only who speaks for the crowd, but who has the *right* to speak for it. Sometimes the gathering is an amorphous group, made up of citizens who are mad about a lot of things—the unfairness of life, their personal frustrations, inflation, unemployment, and the unfathomability of the power structure. The organizers may have skillfully gathered together these disaffected individuals to let off steam. In sum, sometimes a demonstration is not what it seems to be. It may be merely a means to purge the emotions, a catharsis.

The skillful, probing reporter will be sensitive to these nuances, and be clear in his reporting about the *nature* of the protest as against its *billing*. In that way he reveals the human complexity of the occasion along with its political or social dimensions.

Among the questions you should ask individual demonstrators are why are you here? what is happening in your personal life that has led you to join the protest? why did you feel there was no other way to get a fair hearing? what alternative methods have you tried? what is your relationship with the demonstration's organizers? how did you learn about the protest? Of the leaders ask, what are you trying to achieve? why have you chosen this method to send your message? And, most important, what is the specific response you expect?

Always be aware that it is far easier to shout for justice than it is to define it or to make it happen. The reporting needs to move from the powerful emotional impact of people taking to the streets in a democratic society to the painful process of wrestling with the issues. St. Paul told the early Christians that even the Kingdom of God "does not consist in talk but power." (1 Corinthians 4:20) If the purpose of the demonstration is to exercise power, then the reporter has to find out: power to do what? and in whose hands? and in what manner?

Ask whether the target chosen by the demonstrators is an appropriate one. Do they blame city hall when it is the Federal Reserve Board that keeps interest rates high? Do they rail at the Environmental Protection Agency when it is Congress that has just changed the anti-pollution laws? Do they picket the White House when Arab states raise oil prices? For the average citizen living in a society of interlocking, interdependent, and often inscrutable power structures, it may be impossible to ascertain the appropriate target for his protests, but some effort should be made to find that target.

Without a specific target, protests become symbolic gestures, an attempt to attract the attention of those in power, whoever they are, wherever they may be. If you perceive that this is the tenor of the protest, report it. What you have before you could well be something potentially large and of long-term significance instead of an isolated, specifically targeted protest. You may be witness to the kind of grass-roots spasm that heralds deeper and more intractable divisions, the kind that will require drastic and historic political and social responses. The civil rights convulsions and the anti-war demonstrations of the sixties could well have spawned wider social and political revolutions, had the media not appropriately reported them and had the political system not yielded to their demands. Ask yourself whether there are other underground pressures building at this time, and whether this particular demonstration is the tip of that iceberg.

Even as you ruminate on the nature and meaning of the event, you must be making decisions to meet the visual requirements of the medium. To capture the dimensions of the spectacle, where possible the cameraperson should go up to a nearby rooftop or hill and shoot down. This overview can reveal the direction of the march and to what extent the protesters have filled the roadways and overflowed the streets. On the ground, he should shoot pictures of the placards, unusual attire, and the singing, chanting, or silences that can reveal the mood and theme of the event. The variety or homogeneity of individual faces are important pictures, as are nuggets of speeches, and the reactions of the listeners. It is useful to obtain the reactions and comments of bystanders, if any; that is, the interplay between the demonstrating crowd and those outside of it. Symbolic acts like the destruction of images can swiftly and dramatically focus the intent of the demonstrators. (Who among us old enough to remember, can forget the images of Iranians burning President Carter in effigy or veterans tossing their Vietnam war medals on the lawn of the Capitol?) Plainly, when covering a demonstration, you have to be alert to the emotional and symbolic nature of the event as well as its pragmatic implications. However, as you report on it, you must remain apart from it, even when you share a sympathy with the passions and purposes of the participants.

When what begins as a peaceable demonstration becomes a violent civil disturbance, you are confronted with special difficulties directly related to the nature of your medium. The National Advisory Commission on Civil Disorders (The Kerner Commission) reported in 1968 that during the riots of that period most television reporters and camera crews appeared to be aware of the power of the camera to incite trouble, and they behaved with restraint. However, some few egged on the rioters, staged rock-throwing incidents, and encouraged violent behavior in order to obtain action footage. Since that time, responsible news organizations have issued guidelines and warnings to their field teams in an effort to prevent such unethical and unprofessional behavior.

When a demonstration begins quietly and later erupts into violence, how should it be reported? Suppose that the mass of the demonstrators was peaceable and only a few chose to vandalize and break the law? Do you, in your reporting, allow the larger peaceful group to be swallowed up by the dramatic and visual actions of the few? While the reality is that a majority of the demonstrators came peaceably to deliver a message, the incidents of violence can overwhelm that truth if you choose to emphasize them. Be alert to the true nature and temper of the crowd, its purpose and intent, and do not reflexively allow a small group of incendiary troublemakers to shape the way the story emerges. You can tell the story in a sober and quiet fashion, reflecting the peaceful majority, and then, briefly, refer to the trouble. The latter will be relegated to a minor place, if in fact you perceive that it was minor in the total scheme of things.

However, where full-scale civil disorder erupts, there is no way to contain that reality, nor should you try. Plainly the public has the right to know how serious the disturbance is, the parameters of the violence, and what the police and national guard are doing to quell the riot. The causes of the trouble need to be referred to, but in the first-day story, they are likely to take second place to the quality and character of the disturbances themselves.

Be conscious of how difficult it can be to obtain reliable information in a situation of this nature. Rumors, even official rumors, take on a life of their own. What you are likely to get are tiny pieces of the whole picture, some of them filtered through the fears and enlarged imaginations of both law enforcement officers and citizens. To find your way through this tangled thicket, tread warily, and on the whole opt for conservative reporting. That means reporting only what can be fairly confirmed, clearly stating the sources of information and evaluating those sources, and honestly expressing reservations where those exist.

Be aware that, by the very fact of your reporting violence, you may be inspiring violence. You become a part of the event you are covering because what you say can shape the reactions of your viewers to that event. What happens to the public's right to know when the nature of that knowledge can make a situation worse? Is it appropriate for a reporter to hold back information out of consideration for the impact of what he is reporting? In normal times, the reporter believes that he must tell what he knows and let the chips fall where they may. But is this proper in a riot situation? In a revolution? A war?

These are anguishing questions for those who work in print, but they are even more so for television reporters, because of the medium's emotional power and its capacity to inflame.

There are still other questions to be considered. Suppose that the violence represents a justifiable expression of outrage by powerless people? Suppose that the revolutionary forces, however violent, have history and justice on their side? What is the role of the reporter in these circumstances? Does his emphasis on official efforts to contain the troubles in effect place him on the side of the establishment and the status quo? By focusing on law and order, the reporter may project himself as favoring those in power, who have most to lose from the upheaval. By focusing on the protesters, the reporter appears to be sympathetic to that point of view. What is most difficult to achieve here is a semblance of objectivity.

Early demonstrators for civil rights armed themselves with the affecting moral power of nonviolence. The television pictures of Negroes beaten by policemen's clubs and battered by firehoses, became an eloquent and persuasive argument against the injustices heaped upon the country's black people. Major legislation and a revolution in social attitudes soon followed. However, where protesters resort to violence, they are less likely to arouse the same kind of sympathy or to achieve such stunning results. This is so, that is, as long as the television viewer himself feels that change can be effected through nonviolent and legal means. Should the violence on the screen find sympathetic echoes of powerlessness, hopelessness, and rage among sufficient members of the viewing public, then the presence of that violence on television could motivate more citizens to participate.

In a sense, the reporter here finds himself not just an observer of the day's events but a potential participant and animating force as well. The nature of the revolt, its depth, its intent, its power, must all be weighed and evaluated. The reporter must place this convulsion in context, to seek to recognize it as either a momentary aberration or an event that signals something broader and deeper. These perceptions cannot help but affect the way that he sees and reports the story.

Because a demonstration is visually and emotionally arresting, you may be inclined to let the story tell itself. The highly charged nature of the event may tempt you to allow the visuals and the interviews with participants to bear the burden of telling what is happening. This decision would be made at a time when the viewer would perceive that part of his world is coming apart, and he would have a desperate need for explanation. For this reason, among others, where explanation is possible and valid, do not hesitate to include it.

The burden is heavy, especially when you are expected to report live from the scene. How to report soberly on what Queen Elizabeth I once called "those whom reason cannot bridle"? How to explain that seemingly irrational actions can and often do spring from genuine and rationally based grievances? How to explain that, in the search for fairness and equity, those with grievances can be driven to actions that impose unfairness and inequity on other victims (the shopowners, for example, who always seem to bear the brunt of the crowd's arson and fury in America's cities).

It is a tough assignment.

Videotape Editor Tom Engel finishes a story. The editing rooms are adjacent to the news production area, making it easy for everyone to keep track of what is happening.

Anchor Roxanne Stein prepares for a news headline in mid-afternoon.

Economics Editor John Cross delivers his nightly report on business, labor, and the economy from the newscenter.

Reporter Brenda Waters gets in close for interview with Prison official during a hostage drama at a state prison located in Pittsburgh.

During long running story such as this hostage drama, reporters cover in shifts. Here, Vici Rogal on the left gets information from Deborah Pacyna, who has just spent 10 hours covering the story.

Any place will do if there is no chair. Reporter Deborah Pacyna uses curb during prison story.

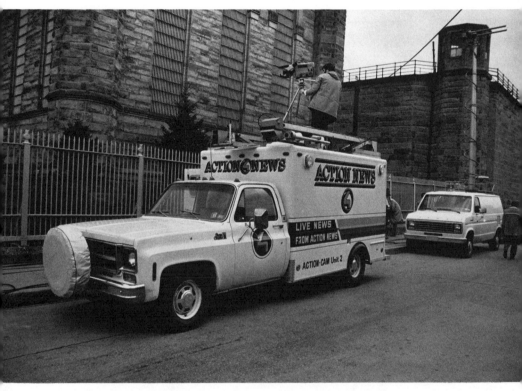

Live ENG trucks crammed with thousands of dollars in equipment, transmitters, and antennae are familiar sites at major news events. Signals are transmitted via microwave back to the station. Reporter must be able to talk smoothly and coherently without benefit of a script in many cases.

CHAPTER TWELVE.

The Art of Interviewing for Television

There are two basic kinds of interview for television: the news interview and the feature interview. Although the skills necessary to conduct these interviews are essentially the same, the goals are different.

For the news interview, the reporter is looking for a brief, focused, and pertinent response to one or two specific questions relevant to a story with a news peg. For the feature interview, the reporter is seeking to reveal the nature and character of the person being interviewed, and the result is likely to be a longer story and soft, less-timely news.

News interviews can occur on the scene of a breaking story or event, or they can be set up in advance. Whatever the circumstance of the interview, the reporter has to be sensitive to the feelings, motives, and sensibilities of the persons involved.

A typical assignment will be the on-the-scene interview at a tragedy of some sort—a fire, an accident, or a murder. You'll be talking with eyewitnesses and with individuals involved in the disaster, including those who have suffered losses. Before you plunge in, take some time to collect your thoughts. The preliminary questions you ask yourself will help to determine the attitude you bring to the scene and the kinds of questions you feel it is appropriate to ask.

Consider the event from the viewpoint of the television viewer. What is it about this particular story that he would want to know or feel the need to know? Put in broader terms and viewed from an alternative perspective, what is the journalist's role when reporting tragedy?

To some extent we consumers of news can be called voyeurs. There exists the perception that we, the public, have the right to know everything, even the most private details of an individual's thoughts, feelings and pains. While newspaper reporters can be nosy and demanding in their efforts to provide these details, the television medium has a greater propensity to intrude in ways that cross the line between decency and bad taste.

Where there is tragedy, the reporter has to sense if and when a grieving individual wants to speak about his grief. Sometimes the individual is paralyzed with shock and he wants to be left alone. His wishes should be respected. On the other hand, some individuals will want to talk. The interview situation helps them to define the nature of their grief by making their pain public and in that way sharing it. Not all television interviews at the scene of tragedies are gratuitous intrusions or breaches of privacy. In many cases the news source welcomes the chance to talk, as though the camera's presence and the interest of the reporter offer some relief from sorrow.

Is this journalism? What does the public need to know about this event? Is it appropriate to explore the pain, grief and tears of those involved in a tragedy?

Journalism has a long tradition of considering tragedy to be the stuff of news. Stories of murder, rape, and arson, auto wrecks and airplane crashes, are news because they are out of the ordinary. They feed the public's need for information, but they also feed some peculiar human attraction to horror. When the tragedy constitutes somebody else's horror, the viewer feels safe and glad that it is the other fellow and not himself who is involved. The viewer shares the pain, but at a distance, all the while relieved because it remains vicarious. "He is dead, I am alive, I am glad that I am the one who lives," is a common feeling at funerals. Or, "There but for the grace of God go I."

Are these reactions callous? Perhaps. But they are also natural and normal sentiments. Tragedy is the stuff of life and art because it heightens our awareness of the irrational and unpredictable nature of the world around us and at the same time impels us to be grateful for our own uneventful lives. The public has the right and need to know about tragedy, but the reporter who reports it must do so with decency and delicacy. The question most commonly misused by television reporters is "How do you feel?" When that question is directed at an individual who has just suffered a grievous loss, it plainly goes beyond what is decent or appropriate.

Questions that are acceptable include those which seek to reconstruct the event and thus help the viewer to understand what happened: When did you first smell the smoke? What went through your mind? What did you do? What happened next? What did you see? What did you do then? These questions are designed to bring out the facts of the situation without gratuitously playing on the emotions. A more indirect and gentler approach would be: "Do you want to tell me about it?" and then leave the person interviewed to talk about whatever he is thinking and feeling at the moment. However, if the response to the latter question is, "No, I don't want to talk about it," then the camera should be turned off and the reporter should leave the individual in peace.

Remember that you must never see the other person as an *object*, that is, as dehumanized material for your television story. While you, as a reporter, have to distance yourself somewhat from everything you see and report, you must not divest yourself of all human concern and compassion. The world is brutal enough without reporters adding to the sum total of its brutality. There exists the danger that, in your hunger for a good story, you will forget what it is to be a caring and considerate human being. Remember that you are the public's representative on the scene, and there are certain kinds of behavior or misbehavior that the public will not tolerate in its delegate, even in the name of getting the news.

There are times when tragedy strikes and the only kind of interview available to you is the group interview. Here, the news source is surrounded by a number of reporters and cameras and the best you can hope for is to ask one of the questions among the many put forward by other reporters. Your camera should be rolling throughout the group interview, but when you are choosing the sound-bite to use in your edited story, apply discretion and good taste. Another reporter may have been cruel and unfeeling in his questioning. Even though his questions have elicited a dramatic response, you may prefer not to use the results of such tasteless techniques, because you believe that you should be setting certain standards for civility and decency. Even in the heat of competition you may prefer to stand by those values.

Many news stories require that you telephone in advance and make an appointment for the interview. How do you persuade a news source to talk to you? Surprisingly, it can be easier than you think. The beginning reporter tends to be in awe of people who hold important positions or those who are well-known. This creates unnecessary inhibitions in pursuit of the story. The only way to find out if somebody will speak with you is to *ask*. Often the public figure is delighted to be asked. He is probably flattered that you thought of him, and glad of the chance to be seen and heard on television.

It will be easier to obtain an interview if you have established a reputation as a reporter who is fair and balanced. If you have instead a reputation for unscrupulousness and ruthlessness, you will no doubt find it harder to persuade a news figure to appear before your camera. This is further evidence that you should develop the respect of your public and your news sources rather than engage in the bloody game of destroy-your-quarry that infects certain overly competitive reporters. However, neither do you want to be perceived as a pussycat whose questions are bland and unchallenging. In that case, you may be granted the interviews, but they will not be worth much when you get them.

Professional politicians, officials, and celebrities, tend to understand the role of the media in public life. They will respect you for doing your job thoroughly, conscientiously, and fairly. With that kind of reputation, doors will open readily.

Suppose that the story you are reporting is one that is likely to cast an unfavorable light on the news source. Do you warn him in advance of the interview? What do you say if he asks you what questions you plan to ask? You can of course reply in vague and general terms. "I want to talk with you about conditions at the city's fire stations," rather than "I want to find out when you began stealing from the firemen's pension fund." Obviously, you are unlikely to gain entree with that last reply. One method is to tell the news source that you have a pretty tough story about him and you plan to go with it, but you think it would be to his advantage to present his side of the question.

Reporters will use a variety of techniques and ruses to get an interview. The key is to refrain from using the tougher tactics unless the story is important enough to merit them. Sometimes the best means at hand is to say that you want to talk about a subject that is dear to the source's heart. Then, once you have settled down with him, you will lead the interview to the matter that is really at issue. You can later justify this apparent digression on the grounds that that is where the interview led you naturally. How can the news source complain about that?

At times your access to the news source will be blocked by a secretary or other intermediary. You telephone again and again, and you are met with the reply, "I'm sorry he is in conference and he cannot be disturbed." There is no effort made to return your calls or respond to messages. In time you get the point that the party does not want to talk with you. If you believe that the interview is important enough to your story, you can take your camera crew to his office and sit in the reception area with your camera at the ready. This ploy has a way of discombobulating some secretaries and lower-level functionaries, and your audacity might just open the door for you. It is possible that you will catch the news source as he is leaving the office, or visiting the rest room. If that's what you are hoping for, make sure there are no alternative exits through which the news source can depart unnoticed.

You may decide to wait for the news source at home. You will park yourself outside of his driveway or down the street, and attempt an interview as he steps out of his car. This is a strong tactic to employ and should not be used unless you have a significant story and this particular news source is vital to it. Some television operations overuse the "ambush interview" in an effort to create drama through confrontation, but this is a singularly inappropriate application of an otherwise valuable technique. The point of the technique is that sometimes a news figure will refuse to be interviewed when you call him on the phone, whereas face to face with the reporter and his camera, the source will bend his rules and agree to talk. A little tenacity on the part of the reporter can pay off.

What do you do if the source says that he will talk with you, but not to the camera? You respect his wishes. Turn the camera off, pull out your notepad, and proceed with the interview. You can then report what he says by quoting him in a stand-up or a voice-over narrative. Even though it is preferable to have the story on videotape, it is the information that counts. Your responsibility is to obtain the information, whatever the shape or form. In fact, many of your best stories will come from telephone interviews where there are no available visuals at all. Visuals are nice, but they remain secondary to substance.

Having lined up the interview, what do you do when you are on the scene? Your first job is to put the news source at ease. You may begin with easy questions, talk about the weather, engage in any kind of chitchat that will show that you are an ordinary fellow human just doing your job.

If the person being interviewed is unaccustomed to the camera, it may take you awhile to persuade him to relax and become less aware of the camera. You can use humor, banter, small talk—whatever you feel will work to put him in the mood to behave naturally in front of the camera.

However, where your interview is with a public figure, you can presume that much of this is unnecessary. Since his time, and yours, is precious, it is best to move directly to the heart of the matter, and then, once you have the information that you need, fold up your equipment and depart. Try not to waste the time of your news subjects, no matter who they are. Your consideration will be much appreciated.

Before you take part in an interview, do your homework. The easiest way to be snowed is to be ignorant of the facts and issues. In the interview situation, the reporter is expected to listen to the news source's replies, and challenge the replies when they seem to be either off-the-track or dissembling. Unless you know even more about the subject than the person you are interviewing, you cannot adequately evaluate or pursue the information that you are receiving. Anything the other fellow says will be accepted by you, and it will not take him long to realize that he is being interviewed by a pushover. As soon as he is wise to this fact, he will be able to manipulate you, saying whatever he pleases and knowing that you are not likely to check out or verify his statements.

Even in the interview situation, it is not the reporter's job to offer a direct pipeline for any official's statement, but rather to apply exacting standards of truth and verification. You cannot absolve yourself with the statement "Well, he said it, didn't he?" Modern journalism requires you to go beyond the news figure's statements to explore their validity and provide the supporting evidence, if there is any. If there is no valid supporting evidence, then the public has the right to know that.

This bitter lesson was learned the hard way by reporters and editors involved in the coverage of Senator Joseph McCarthy in the 1950s Cold War period. At that time, the Wisconsin Republican was spearheading a virulent anti-communism that was later recognized as an undemocratic witchhunt. Using a Senate committee as a platform, McCarthy made wild and unsubstantiated charges against government employees, actors, journalists, and other citizens, and in the process he ruined many lives. McCarthy's pronouncements were reported almost without challenge by a press that then believed its only responsibility was to report what was being said. The simple fact that the Senator was saying what he was saying became news and big news. The failure of the media, at least in the early stages of the McCarthy phenomenon, to examine the truth or falsehood of the charges gave to the Senator unfettered power to destroy reputations without fear of retribution or challenge. It was only later that reporters and editors came to realize how they had been used as a vehicle to promote falsehoods. After some soul-searching, a different standard of journalism developed: the press should not merely report what someone says, but should tell the public to the best of its ability whether those statements can be substantiated.

Normally, a public figure will prefer to be interviewed by a reporter who understands the subject matter. The interview can then develop into something more than a routine question-and-answer exercise. It becomes instead a conversation between two well-briefed, intelligent human beings. One of the highest compliments the reporter can receive after an interview is to be told, "You were tough, but I enjoyed that." Often the individual you are interviewing will sharpen and refine his ideas because of your probing, and he will be grateful for the test.

Approach the news source without being either subservient or aggressive. Where you come to the occasion well-briefed and where your attitude is that of an equal, you are likely to be treated with respect. So will the public, whom you are representing. If the news subject has nothing to hide, if in fact he has thought through his positions in logical and intelligent fashion, then your probing will place him in a good light. Where your questions reveal flaws, weaknesses and evasions, you will have prompted him to tighten up his research and analysis. A good interview can be an education for both the interviewer and the interviewee.

When preparing for an interview, it is not enough simply to know a great deal about the subject at hand. A good interviewer must be widely informed on many subjects. Read your newspaper thoroughly that morning, and develop the habit of reading and thinking on a continuing basis. A reply from the news subject during an interview can relate to another issue that is timely, or it can indicate a pattern of thinking that reflects on other seemingly non-related issues. This response will trigger a series of questions that you may not have expected to ask, but the results can lead to a wealth of fresh material.

During the interview, listen to the answers and make connections in your mind, leading the interviewee to relate his just-made statement to its possible implications for other matters. In this way, a good interview can move well beyond the predictable by peeling away the surface masks to reveal what is underneath.

On occasion, during feature interviews, the reporter *appears* to be extracting honesty, but instead he settles for a counterfeit candor—small facts clev-erly shaped in forms that adapt comfortably to the medium. The good in-terviewer is painfully aware that facts and truth are not synonymous, that they may in fact be strangers to each other. The interviewed actor, movie star, or author, often appears to be confessional, but in fact he or she is giving the performance of his or her life. A certain skepticism, a gentle "Aw, come on now," may be necessary to cut through the maudlin garbage. The news subject may be playing games, testing the reporter, trying to find out how much stuff-and-nonsense the reporter is willing to accept. The control of the interview should rest in the reporter's hands. If the news subject gains the upper hand, it becomes a farce.

Bring to any interview a list of prepared questions. The process of writing them down will help you to refine your thinking and shape the direction that you want the interview to take. However, do not lock yourself into a preprogrammed interview, where you reel off your prepared questions in order, without listening to, or reacting to, the answers you receive. You have to listen closely in order to follow up, bounce off, and pick up themes and threads that are worth pursuing. Flexibility is vital to an interview situ-ation. In sum, you can and must prepare by doing preliminary research and preparing questions, but once you are in the interview situation it is what you are and who you are and how you think that will shape the ensuing exchange.

A word of advice: remember that you are the reporter and it is the other fellow who is the object of the interview. The public is not particularly interested in your opinions. The viewer wants to hear from the news figure. While you need to exercise control, you must remember that you are the supporting cast and not the star and keep your intrusions minimal. Further-more, in a videotaped interview if you step on or talk over the last words of the news subject's answer, it will make it difficult to edit the story. Allow the source to finish his sentence before you move on to the next question, *unless* he is filibustering and you do not intend to use that answer anyhow. Sometimes it will be necessary to jump in and move the subject back on track and there is simply no other way to control the situation.

There are many kinds of questions that can be asked during an interview. The basic kinds are informational. What? How many? When? Where? Then there are questions that are explanatory. Why? To what purpose? How do you account for? What went into your deliberations? How did you weigh the arguments for the other side?

There are questions designed to elicit anecdotal material. How did you first learn? What was your reaction? What did you do then? Who said what? And there are questions that try to set the information in a broader context. What effect will this have on specific groups of people? How do you reconcile this decision with your other decisions? What are its implications for politics or foreign affairs or social change? Does this offer evidence of a philosophical shift? And personal questions: What did you give up in order to succeed in your career? Have you any regrets? How did your success affect your relations with your spouse, your children? What made you choose this path and not another? How does the public spotlight affect your view of yourself?

Plainly there are as many kinds of questions as there are interviews, and the reporter's capacity to ask the right questions will depend on his personal curiosity, intelligence, and sense of what news is.

Try to frame your questions succinctly. This is not always easy because you may be fumbling for precision. A practiced television interviewer will avoid setting up a question by means of a lengthy, tortured introduction.

Do not ask double-barrelled questions. Ask one question at a time so that you receive one answer at a time. The results will be easier for the public to follow and the reply will be easier to edit. You can then proceed to follow up on a single answer before moving on to the next question. Remember that an effective piece of journalism will lay out the subject matter clearly point by point. When you ask two questions in a single inquiry you are likely to receive a tangled response.

Do not be afraid to appear stupid. There are times when the person you are interviewing will employ jargon or deal opaquely with complex material. You can quite properly interject and say, "I'm sorry, but I don't understand. Could you please explain that in simple language?" You owe it to the viewer to do this because he will probably be even more baffled than you are. You, at least, have had time to research the subject before the interview. The poor television viewer is sitting at home and coming to the subject cold turkey. It is perfectly all right to admit your ignorance in order to obtain clarification and explanation.

Sometimes during an interview, the news subject will refer to something or somebody that you know the public is unlikely to understand. You should jump in and say something like, "Oh, by that you mean——" or "I think you are referring to——" and thus explain the reference on the spot. Avoid using a reply which will require later explanation in the middle of the interview. If you have to use that particular sound-bite, you can follow it with an explanation in the stand-up or voice-over. However, this is a complicating and unnecessarily confusing technique. It is best to press the person interviewed to explain his references when they occur, or for you to explain them in an interpolation. Remember that while you may understand the reference the viewer may not, and your role in the interview is to make things clear to the viewer.

The feature interview requires of the reporter additional in-depth research. If you have the time, you should try to contact friends, acquaintances and colleagues of the interviewee, in search of background, insights, and anecdotes that will enrich your dialogue. You will want to read what has been said about the news subject in the past. You may even talk with the interviewee's enemies. Armed with this kind of material, should you find the news subject telling a self-serving story, you might say, "Well, that's not the way so-and-so tells it." That indication from you that you have been doing your homework will bring the interviewee up sharp and perhaps inspire him to be somewhat more accurate in his responses.

A word that you will hear in discussions of the interview process is *rapport*. When you establish rapport with the news subject you are making a connection—that is, you are building mutual trust and respect. Most of the barriers between you are removed. It is easier to achieve this goal with some interviewees than it is with others. The reporter's confidence, good humor, tact, and sensitivity have to be brought into play here, and as in so much of human relations, you have to simpy play each occasion by ear. There are no firm guidelines that will apply to every situation.

The television interview can be videotaped for later editing or it may be live and unedited. Obviously the live interview is risky, because you cannot cover up your goofs by editing them out. However, on the plus side, the unedited interview has a natural flow to it that is very attractive when well-handled. The viewer is able to see the progression from one idea to the next and to hear the complete replies from the news source. Whether the interview is taped or live, follow up on answers that plainly require more probing. However, in the live interview a glaring failure to follow up can cause the attentive viewer some consternation. He will be left with questions in his head, questions that you failed to raise, and you will leave him with an unsatisfied feeling.

One of the traps of live interviewing is to be caught planning your next question when you should be listening to what the interviewee is saying in response to your last one. Sometimes you are planning to move on to the next topic but you move too soon, before the former subject has been adequately explored. In the live interview, you also have to be aware of the time—watch the signals from the floor manager, pace yourself so that you cover the ground you want to cover before the time runs out.

If your time is limited, it helps to do a preliminary warmup to relax the person you will be interviewing before you go on the air. That way you do not have to spend on-air time for nonessential conversation. However, be careful not to ask your key questions during the warmup. You should save those for the program so that the on-air responses are fresh and unrehearsed.

The live interview requires that the reporter exercise considerable mental organization and control. Some experienced public figures will try to take over the interview, leading it into areas that interest them but not you, giving you long answers to questions you never asked, and generally trying to use up the time on self-serving statements while keeping you from getting to the crucial questions that you want to pose. The effective interviewer will politely and firmly nip this activity in the bud. You might allow the news subject one answer of this kind on his own terms, but after that, if he continues to filibuster, barge in and say, "I'm sorry, sir, but you aren't answering my question. Let me repeat it." Make sure that you will not run out of time before you get to the heart of the enterprise. The central issues must be addressed and the responses followed up if the live interview is to have a point or value.

When you are approaching the end of your air time, avoid asking a complex question that is likely to require a lengthy answer. It helps to have prepared in advance a question that is likely to evince a brief and pointed reply. You can then close the interview neatly, without having to cut off your news subject in mid-sentence. If, however, time has run out and you are forced to interrupt, do so when he is taking a breath or has ended a sentence or a phrase. Smile, shrug, and say, "I'm sorry, but it seems our time has run out. I want to thank you" and so on.

In preparation for terminating the interview, some reporters will explain to the news subject before they go on the air what the final signals will be and what will be expected of the interviewee at that point. Another approach is to say on-air, "We have just thirty seconds. Let me ask you this"—remarks which will indicate to the interviewee that he should get to his point quickly and succinctly.

If you can manage to tie up a live interview neatly and gracefully, you will leave the viewer with the feeling that the interview had a beginning, a middle, and an end, as well as a point and a purpose.

CHAPTER THIRTEEN.
Dealing With Officials

Much of the news that journalists report is based on the words of officials. It is appropriate that news organizations cover government leaders because they have so much power over citizens' lives. However, at times it seems that reporters cover government to the virtual exclusion of other (private) institutions, like banks, universities, corporations, labor unions, and foundations, which are powerful, too. There is a tendency to hold government more accountable than private institutions, even where the decisions of institutions have enormous impact on the society around them. A journalism that consistently ignores these private centers of power is an inadequate source of public information, but there are reasons why most of journalism focuses on government.

Private institutions can be reluctant to reveal information about their activities. Nor do they feel obliged to disclose how or why they make decisions. The Freedom of Information Act, which requires that government agencies disclose nonclassified information to an inquiring public, does not affect private institutions. It is more difficult for a reporter to obtain information from private avenues and thus he turns to government officials as the chief source of his news.

However, even where reporters do cover government, they tend to concentrate on certain well-known and "glamorous" divisions, while virtually ignoring others. As a result of this lopsided attention, some significant government work is done away from the prying eyes of reporters, while other areas have a surfeit of reporters pursuing them. These same "glamorous" divisions usually know how to keep the media happy. However, what ends up being reported can be less real news than ballyhoo.

For example, in Washington, hundreds of reporters crowd into the White House press room daily, waiting for what is jocularly termed "the four o'clock feeding of the fishes." These are the four o'clock briefings by the White House Press Secretary, followed by the distribution of often banal and trivial publicity handouts that are eagerly snapped up by the crowd. Certainly, there is significant news that emanates from the Presidency. But most of it is stock, predigested information that could more efficiently be left to a handful of newswire reporters to report on and file. The rest of the reporters would do better to disperse in pursuit of the inner workings of key committees of Congress, departments like Agriculture and Labor, and regulatory agencies like the Federal Communications Commission and the Nuclear Regulatory Commission. Although these committees, departments and agencies affect the everyday lives of citizens in important ways, most are poorly covered unless there is a crisis.

These comments on the way the federal government is unevenly covered, apply as readily to state, county, and local governments. A new reporter could eventually carve out a good beat for himself by making contact with sources inside the lesser-known and underreported areas of government. However, in the beginning, the new reporter is likely to find himself assigned to cover the traditional, readily available official. When he gets that assignment, the intelligent reporter will analyze the role of the official, separating the appearance of his power from its reality.

He will note, for example, that even though the Mayor is declaring he will do this or that, in fact, the Mayor has little power to effect change without the support of the long-entrenched city bureaucracies. Union contracts, work-rules, civil service regulations, uncooperative bureaucrats, can turn the best-laid mayoral plans to dust. It is important for a reporter to explain to the public the relationship between the public *intentions* of an official, and the realistic possibilities for change. It is misleading to leave the impression that, simply by virtue of the Mayor's having said it, it will happen.

Recent polls indicate that a considerable number of citizens are soured on government. And no wonder. Again and again the journalist has trumpeted official promises and then failed to link them with productive action. By giving so much attention to words, reporters can leave the impression that all that officials have to do is pass a law, or make a speech, and voila! The problem is solved. Later, when it dawns on the citizen that in spite of all the talk, passage of bills, and expenditure of taxpayer money, nothing much has changed, he feels angry and cheated.

Contextual journalism—that is, reporting an event against the background necessary to understand and evaluate it—is rare enough in the print medium. In local television, alas, it is virtually unknown.

In local television news, often the story about an official is covered because the official is prominent, he is easily available, or the story will be presented in a way designed to catch the eye of the camera. An artfully written press release that promises visual enticements is bound to attract representatives from local television stations, especially on a day when not much else is happening. This effort to bring the suckers into the tent usually works because local television news is a willing sucker. Even network news crews have been known to fall for similar devices, especially where the President is involved.

Whether all of this is news or not is one question. Whether other more important stories are going unreported because of it is another, and more serious, one. Government officials know that one way to get the public's mind off real problems is to create a diversion. When journalists unquestioningly play along with this tactic, they are failing to live up to their public responsibilities.

It's plain from the above that to describe government and the media as adversaries is to oversimplify a complex relationship. If you inspect that relationship closely, you will find more symbiosis than conflict. Government officials need the media to get their stories across. The media need the officials in order to gain access to government and to report on it. Each uses and often manipulates the other. Most of the time, each side knows what it is doing, why it is doing it, and how far it will allow itself to be used. Whatever happens to the search for truth and the public's right to know in this game is a question for philosophers. The sad thing is that, while sophisticated television viewers may instinctively understand how the game is played, unsophisticated ones will buy the charade and consider it real.

How, then, should a reporter approach the task of covering an official? The answer is—warily. In perhaps no other journalistic territory is it so important that the reporter remain aware of what his professional responsibility requires of him. For the new reporter, it is often exciting and ego-inflating to find himself close to power. There is a need to be noticed, to be liked, to attract the attention of the top banana. It is perfectly okay to move in quickly, to make your mark. One of the things you will want and need is access, and while some public officials are readily available to almost anyone, others tend to distribute access as favors to the reporters or news organizations that they like.

Your problem here is to get yourself liked enough to gain access, but not so much that you find yourself co-opted. This is a difficult line to walk. One of the first things that you can do is to keep a certain distance. Do NOT, under any circumstances, call the public figure by his first name. Use the title. If he wants to call you Robyn, that's his problem. But you should (gently) make it plain that he is not your buddy or your pal, but somebody who is paid with the people's tax money and therefore somebody you must report about fairly, honestly, and, yes, even harshly at times.

Smart politicians will try to flatter you in order to win you over to their side. The flattery may be overt—like a nice comment on last night's story, or a compliment on your hair, or your smile. The flattery may be in the form of so-called "exclusives," or leaked documents "I'm giving to you only." The naïve reporter will consider himself on the inside now, and will become an easy mark for the practiced politician who wants a direct conduit to the public. Charm is laid on in thick dollops, and charm combined with political power is an awesome weapon in the hands of a master. Some of the reporters who covered President John F. Kennedy now confess that there were a number of stories they did not tell about him and his policies simply because they liked him and were charmed by him.

Journalism is an imperfect art, and when the reporter forgets who he is and why he is there—when he fuzzes up the difference between a personal relationship and a professional relationship—he can lose his capacity to be impartial, cool, and tough.

Sometimes a new reporter figures that the best way for him to establish himself is to be mean and nasty, rude and sneering. Television reporters are particularly prone to this disease because their meanness, nastiness, rudeness, and sneers can be seen (and perhaps, they think, applauded) by the viewing public. This kind of reporter will use every opportunity to confront the public figure, embarrass him, and engage him in verbal combat. Here is the other extreme of reporter behavior. It bears little relationship to journalism, and fails miserably to serve the public's right to information and understanding. Furthermore, in the long run it is self-defeating, because any public figure so humiliated and ill-treated is hardly likely to respect or trust that particular reporter with important information. For the system to work, there must be some trust on both sides, as well as mutual respect.

A good politician understands "where a reporter is coming from." He appreciates reporters' moral imperatives, mindset, duties, and responsibilities. The good reporter understands that the view from the other side is different, that political figures have their own purposes, interests, and operating rules. While it is true that no one in public office acts entirely without self-interest, neither does the reporter. The public figure wants to present his case in the best possible light, for political reasons. The reporter wants to beat out the competition, get a pat on the head from the boss, and inform the public. If you understand the motives as well as the modus operandi of each side, you'll be able to keep the relationship in perspective.

In sum, you should approach an official wanting neither to be loved nor hated. You will want him to respect your professionalism, and in turn you must do the same. It is a game, but a serious one, because what is at stake is public opinion. The public official may want to conceal more than he reveals, and that's the way he plays his checkers. The reporter will want to reveal rather than allow the official to conceal, and he will use assorted strategies to obtain the information that he wants.

For the television reporter it is often difficult to do the kind of patient, slogging journalism that leads to revelations of important information. Usually, the demand on him is to get something quick, get it visual, and stick it on the air that same night. While the camera can be a blessing in some circumstances, it is a handicap in others. The basic work of journalism should precede the visual demands. The reporter needs to make contacts, talk with middle-level bureaucrats who probably know more than the man at the top, read documents, talk with citizens and with lawyers involved in the issues. Much of this kind of work is best done without a camera, and yet often the television reporter is expected to belly up with his electronic gear—a tactic that may scare off those who are likely to know what's going on. Patient, quiet legwork of the old-fashioned kind can pay off with better stories, if only local stations would free reporters on occasion to practice it.

Even if you have to do it on your own time, develop quiet contacts with key officials. The television reporter who meets an official in a general news conference and nowhere else, is at a disadvantage. The signs of shift and change—a turn of direction—which would be noticed by somebody who has observed the official on a regular basis will be lost on the reporter who dashes into a news conference, videotapes a short sound-bite, and then departs. The subtleties, the inner meanings, the finer points, will remain unnoticed and unreported. One is left instead with surface journalism, wham-bang journalism, empty stuff, not particularly worthy of the viewer's time and attention.

Never underestimate the power of an official to manipulate, hide, deceive, or dissemble. On the other hand, don't presume that all officials are in the business of hiding things or lying. Approach the official with a cool "show-me" attitude: neither obsequious, nor pugnacious. Your attitude should be "I'm here doing my job. You're there doing your job. Now let's get on with it as best and amicably as we can."

Be attentive. Be respectful. Listen carefully, not just to what is said, but to what remains unsaid. Where you hear jargon or bureaucratic mumbo-jumbo, smile sweetly and ask for clarification, explanation, and plain talk. You can disarm the official by admitting your need for simplification and clarity. You usually can win more with honey than with vinegar, but sometimes the only recourse you have is vinegar. Don't be afraid to use it if you have to.

Do not accuse the official of lying, cheating, or incompetence, even if you suspect him of one or all of these failings. Ask him the kind of questions that force him to come to terms with the specifics of the cases and issues at hand. Peel away the outer layers of generalities. If he offers you a general statement like, "We treated that welfare client fairly," ask him to tell you in what specific ways did he do so. In sum, you are trying to get to the facts, the nitty-gritty, of the story, and you have to be sure you are not snowed by fancy language and artful footwork. Too many reporters—in particular local television reporters—content themselves with the first glib answer to a question, and fail to dig beneath it, where the real information lies buried.

A serious obstacle to the work of a television journalist lies in the perception that the only story worth having is the one in which an official will go on the record and talk directly to the camera. This approach to news can seriously limit the quality and character of the stories the reporter produces. The official who is likely to gain access to the reporter's slice of the airwaves will thus be the one who relishes being in the public eye, the one who wants to promote himself. This official may also recognize that, by being accessible he can get his story across in a fashion that suits his own purposes.

Ask yourself: why is this guy so readily available? What's in it for him?

How does his presence on camera serve the public's right to know *what is really happening?* And, by making himself so available, what other voices are NOT being heard on this issue?

Senior government officials want information about their agencies to come from themselves or from routine, public-information channels. They worry about leaks from mid- and lower-level bureaucrats who probably know a great deal more about how the official's public statements translate into action. They also worry about disgruntled and disaffected bureaucrats who may choose to leak a story to the media and thus upset the neat public image projected by the man at the top.

How does a television reporter handle a leak? Usually, the leaker will not agree to be videotaped on camera. Sometimes the information leaked can be elicited from another source. In other words, knowing what you know without being able to reveal the source, you try to find another source who *will* talk on camera.

If this process fails, the reporter is faced with a story that will be based on sources he cannot publicly identify. He then has the task of carefully checking the veracity and reliability of the source, and of authenticating the information in the leak. He should be alert to the possibility of misinformation—that is, information that is simply wrong—and disinformation—stories planted maliciously to confuse and confound the public. However, if the story proves to be a good one, and the news director gives the go-ahead, the reporter can present his report as a "tell" story, without videotaped material. He may use supporting documents as visuals, as well as art work, still photos, and graphics.

Why does anyone in government choose to leak to the media? You should undertake to find out the motives of the leaker, in order to evaluate him as a source. For example, there are official leaks, the kind that come straight from the top. When Henry Kissinger was Secretary of State, he made it a practice to leak stories to members of the media who were traveling with him on his trips around the world. Stories would be filed citing "highly placed officials," but in fact the source was the Secretary of State himself. The reason for the deception was this: in the culture of diplomacy, when a Secretary of State goes on the record, what he says bears the full weight of official government policy. However, a story attributed to "highly placed official sources" can prompt public debate, stir the opposition to show its hand, and generally serve as a trial balloon, without pinning the administration down to a specific policy. In other words, the government official, in this case the Secretary of State, can test the waters for a policy under consideration, while remaining free to change the policy if it is found to be too risky.

Why does the press agree to go along with this kind of manipulation? Clearly it is a legitimate form of cooperation between media and government if the information so revealed gives to the public, and other officials, access to the thinking and tentative plans of high officials. What is less palatable is the phoniness of the procedure, and the deception of the public. Furthermore, official leaks of this nature can be (and sometimes are) subsequently denied by the very officials who leaked them, and since the reporters feel honor-bound not to reveal the source, they are left with the unhappy problem of their shaken credibility.

A leak can be used by one official to discredit or embarrass another official who opposes his policies. Mid-level bureaucrats who do not like certain government policies have been known to leak information that will put those policies in a bad light. Sometimes the motive for a leak is to force a reaction from higher officials in the same organization or from elsewhere in government. As government divisions grow larger and more isolated from each other, some bureaucrats use leaks as a means of attracting the attention of other bureaus. If the story breaks on the evening news or in the morning papers, the other bureau is going to have a hard time ignoring it.

Sometimes the leak comes from a genuine, concerned whistle-blower, an individual inside government whose conscience is stung by what he sees, and who feels that public exposure could help to set things right. But there are many traps in using leaked material, and any reporter on the verge of doing so should be wary. Sometimes only partial documents are leaked. Information that might contradict the story as the leaker wants it told is withheld from the reporter. Remember that leaked information can be unfair to an individual who is being accused, but who cannot know the name of his accuser. And remember, too, that somebody who leaks a good story may want you to reward him later by running another story. There may be no harm in this kind of bargain, but whenever a reporter finds himself under *obligation* to a news source, he runs the risk of being compromised.

Plainly, one must be particularly careful about using leaked material. On the whole, it is best to persuade your source to go on the record, because in the end a story that can be attributed carries more weight.

Officials are increasingly wise in the ways of the media, and they often time their news conferences, hearings, and announcements to meet the media's deadlines and demands. For example, Saturdays and Sundays are notoriously slow news days. A government official is likely to win rather complete coverage of a news conference if he schedules it on either of those two days. If what he says is even minimally newsworthy, it may even be on the front page of next day's newspapers and lead the television news that evening. Scheduled for another day, when it must compete against the speeches and activities of other officials, the story could well be lost entirely.

Furthermore, savvy officials know that anything that happens after four o'clock is going to have to be fairly significant if it is to be covered, and they will schedule their announcements at an earlier hour. However, if the story is highly controversial, timing the conference for the later hour will probably preclude the media from obtaining opposing viewpoints in time to meet their deadlines. Thus, the official's pronouncements are almost guaranteed a solo flight on the air and in the next day's papers, because the reporter doesn't have time to present the other side. Some allusion to this fact in the news story would not be inappropriate, because it would tell the viewer why the opposition is not heard from at this time.

Another way that officials manage the news is to choose which reporters they will invite to participate in an event. If the new reporter finds himself unaccountably invited to represent his organization on an official tour or at a select news conference of reporters, he should not automatically feel flattered. It may be that the official who invited him prefers to have the scene surveyed and the questions raised by a naïve reporter—one likely to be ignorant of the history, significance, and subtle meanings of what's going on. This is one way that an official can end-run the tough-minded, seasoned beat reporter who has been close to the story for a long time. The skeptical reporter is denied access. The innocent one gets the invitation. A new reporter who finds himself in this position will touch base with the seasoned reporter for backgrounding before he attends the event. Armed with substantive information, he may even surprise the official with his unexpected knowledge and wisdom on the issues at hand. Of course, the result may be that you'll never be invited back again, but that's a price you may be willing to pay to let the official know that you are wise to his game.

If from all of the above, you gather that the relation between reporters and officials is a complicated one, you will be right. Sometimes you are working *with* the official—willingly accepting information from him and transmitting it to the public. At other times, you are making life difficult for the official by challenging his statements, and by reporting on criticisms and responses from people with opposing views. Games are played by both reporters and officials, each side trying to win according to his perception of his role and his responsibility.

Ever since the Watergate period, certain segments of the media have become bloodthirsty in their efforts to expose, destroy, and embarrass public officials. Some of the activity described as "investigative reporting" is petty and insignificant, and constitutes harassment.

A decent sense of the need for good men and women to take on the responsibilities and frustrations of governing should help to temper these unpleasant and at times ugly media attitudes. However, it would be wrong to argue for a return to the McCarthy era, when the media were almost supine in their acceptance of official statements as gospel truth. Some balance and perspective are desperately in order.

For government officials in a democratic system, the support of the public is important to success. The reporter plays a central role in the official's ability to win that support. To do his job well, the reporter needs to understand the nature and limitations of the power that the official holds. He needs to understand the pressures, the frustrations, and the temptations involved in the job the official does. But he needs always to keep in mind that he serves neither the official nor himself. He serves as the people's watchdog—and much depends on how well or badly he exercises his skill as a dispassionate observer and recorder of official actions as well as official words.

CHAPTER FOURTEEN.

Covering People Other Than Officials

A government official whose salary is paid by the taxpayer can avoid the media if he so chooses. But he opens himself to considerable criticism if he does so when there are issues at stake that affect the public. When you approach an official, you are armed with a certain rightness, if not quite righteousness, on your side. Anybody paid by public monies is fair game in the contest between press and government.

However, when you are reporting on people who are not officials, your right to access is less clear. The individual can, if he so chooses, simply refuse to speak with you. He can say he is a private citizen, and he wishes to remain private, and if you try to breach that privacy without his permission, he can sue.

Sometimes, however, a private citizen is also a public figure, and in that case he has less right to privacy than Mr. Smith or Ms. Jones who lives around the corner. When an individual accepts a role as a leader in such nongovernmental fields as business or education, he is no longer "ordinary" and the reporter may be forgiven for raising the level of his persistence and tenacity in pursuit.

However, much of television journalism requires that the reporter interview citizens who play no official or public roles. These citizens will come from a variety of educational backgrounds, experiences and races and include all manner of beliefs and attitudes. The reporter has to learn how to approach each of them and draw from them the information he needs.

The attitude that the reporter brings to the person he is covering can to a great extent determine the success he will have in persuading the individual to talk, and to talk honestly and freely. Some reporters use bluster and intimidation to persuade people to talk to the cameras. They rush forward, microphone in hand, asking outrageous, even insulting, questions. They like to make their quarry angry, in the hope that, in anger, the truth will out. Sometimes this technique works. More often what emerges is a nasty, unseemly exchange that is emotional rather than informative. The individual so challenged is caught off guard, and is likely to show up in a bad light if he exhibits the slightest anger or ill humor.

Some reporters enjoy casting the other person in a bad light, because it establishes them as tough guys who won't be pushed around. Sadly, there are a few television managements that approve of, and even encourage, this behavior, on the grounds that their reporters can thus become established as memorable personalities who will attract viewers to the program. What any of this has to do with the duties and responsibilities of a reporter in terms of *informing* the public, it's hard to say.

However, sometimes you have to be tough to get your story. If a key figure has been avoiding you or stonewalling, you may have to resort to guerrilla tactics. But such techniques should be reserved for important stories and information that is both central and unobtainable in any other way. Even so, you should maintain a professional presence and treat the news subject with dignity and respect.

At the other end of the spectrum, some reporters are too easily dissuaded from pursuing an interview. The first "no" sends them into retreat, and in the process, many excellent opportunities are lost. There are occasions when the first "no" is merely reflex, or it may reflect shyness. The average citizen may say, who, me? why me? and send you on your way. With only a tiny bit of persistence, you might well be able to persuade the same individual that yes, indeed, he is important enough to warrant interest.

Plainly, there are as many kinds of interview and story situations as there are stories, and the good reporter has to be exceedingly sensitive to the nuances of circumstance and individual behavior. You may want to flatter the interview subject. You may want to persuade him that he is important, that what he has to say really counts. You may want to play upon his wish to make a difference, to shape events. You may want to argue gently that, by speaking out, he will be doing a public service, and helping other people. In short, you must be something of an amateur psychologist, searching for the key to unlock the door.

Remember that the camera itself can be intimidating. To someone who is unused to the equipment and the technicians, and to the idea of having himself revealed and recorded, it can be terrifying to be confronted by the prospect of a television interview. To ease the way for the interviewee, be pleasant, friendly, and disarming. Make an effort to present the occasion as something not so extraordinary after all.

Remember that, the very fact that you are a television reporter, perhaps a reporter whose face is familiar to the individual you are talking to, can cause that person to freeze. You're NOT simply Robyn Smith, person, but Robyn Smith, THE TV reporter. It's your task to sell yourself as "just folks," an ordinary person, stripped of glamor, stepped down from the TV pedestal. If you are going to establish rapport, you need to remember that a TV reporter who becomes entrapped in her own celebrity, can destroy her capacity to talk with citizens from all walks of life.

Don't talk down to people. You need to speak in simple, direct, unacademic fashion, using words that the other person can understand. At the same time you have to be careful not to patronize. The average citizen is smarter than you think.

Your first task will be to help the news source to relax. A bit of humor helps, but so does a relaxed attitude on your part. If you are all a-bustle and a-worry, your tensions will be transmitted to the person you are trying to interview, and he will end up feeling nervous. You need to establish your common humanity with the interviewee, but it should be on a level that will make it possible for both of you to communicate calmly and thoughtfully.

Your job will require that you draw out the person, but you should be careful not to plant ideas, or put words in his mouth. There is always a danger that, having prepackaged the video story in your head, you know what sound-bite you want, and you are determined to get it—*even if that's not what the interviewee wants to say.*

This is television journalism at its worst. Crude. Manipulative. No doubt you have seen this happen on the air. The reporter says, "You feel angry, don't you?"

"Yes, I do."

"And you want to get back at him, right?"

"Yes, that's right."

"And you're going to find a way to get back at him?"

"I sure am."

What's wrong here is that, as any lawyer would put it, the reporter is "leading the witness." He is shaping his questions in such a way that the interviewee is persuaded to go along. Furthermore, the questions are framed so as to elicit a yes-or-no answer, instead of complete statements in the words of the person interviewed.

The same information can be obtained by asking: "How do you feel?" "What do you want to do about it?" "What are you *going* to do?" If the interviewee is angry and plans revenge, the reporter will have obtained that information, but in a more honorable form than in the previous exchange.

However, the reporter could be in for a surprise. The person interviewed may not be angry, may not feel vengeful—may in fact feel compassion, or sorrow, or forgiving. That unexpected response will naturally mess up the reporter's preplanned TV package. The reporter is faced with the fact that news is not something that can be scripted like a play. The reporter is expected to go with the story the way it falls in place, and not the way he has projected it in his head.

Some reporters are so determined to shape the video package in the way they want it, that they will rehearse segments of the interview or the event. They become captives of the medium, and the honesty of the message be damned. This is both unethical and immoral, and is grounds for dismissal at better television stations.

However, some critics of television news stretch the term "rehearsal" too far. It is *not* rehearsing when you ask a person to answer the same question in briefer form. You are not putting words in his mouth, or changing what he says. You are asking him to say it again, in his own way, but to keep it short. It is like asking a writer to edit himself to fit his words into a smaller space—a perfectly acceptable practice, so long as one does not ask that the substance of the material be changed, too.

The average reporter tends to be sympathetic with the little guy, and there's nothing wrong with that—*unless* it gets in the way of his professional objectivity. You have to verify and authenticate information, even when it comes from a sympathetic source. Little guys do lie, you know. Like officials, they want to look good in front of the camera, and you have to apply as strict a yardstick in measuring their veracity as you do to those who hold powerful positions.

How do you do this without scaring the person away? You ask for specifics, for evidence, for proof, but you do it without being prosecutorial. "I'm just doing my job, ma'am," is the appropriate approach. Generalities and opinions have their place in news, but the real meat and potatoes of any news story lies with facts and specifics. Too much television deals in sound and fury that signifies nothing. The story that is grounded in detail and proof adds something real to the public's store of information and understanding.

Again, you have to remember why you are doing what you are doing. It is no more your purpose to get on the right side of the little guy than it is to get on the right side of the bigwig. It is your job to probe, to uncover what lies buried, to shed light on dark corners. You have to ask penetrating questions. You have to ask the right questions. You have to make the person you are interviewing confront his realities instead of his wishes.

Some individuals enjoy playing the role of victim. It is easier to blame one's parents and background, and even society as a whole, instead of oneself. The idea that the individual shares some responsibility for his own predicament has not exactly been a popular one in recent times. Much of news reporting is based on the presumption that every event has a purely *social* cause. This mindset can trap the reporter into searching for an official scapegoat when in fact there is none.

If you ask an ordinary citizen in trouble whom he blames for his condition, he's likely find something or someone to blame. But if you ask him instead for a detailed report on how he got where he is, what he did, what he didn't do, you are more likely to reach a truth. This is not to argue against the proposition that many personal troubles spring from social and political causes. It is merely to state that you should not automatically presume that is the key element in every story. Life is more complex than that, and we demean a person's uniqueness and individuality when we turn him into a mere creature of social forces.

Television has enormous power to reveal the individuality of people, the complexity of the real world, and the way that social forces interact with the individual. The reporter who approaches the ordinary citizen in search of social scapegoats oversimplifies reality, and mutilates truth. An intelligent and balanced sense of both the power and the limitations of politics and social action to effect change will help the reporter to bring maturity and responsibility to his reporting.

The right degree of skepticism is applicable to all the people you come in contact with, and it will apply as well to some of our modern sacred cows. The idea that the way to solve problems is to spend lots of money on them is a case in point. The best reporter refuses to react as a kneejerk liberal or conservative. He sees that things are shifting and changing, that old ideas that seemed good at the time may not be working now, that new ways of looking at things are called for. If he wants to do his job right, he will free himself from the collective mentality, and raise the kinds of questions that will attack issues and problems from different, even unexpected angles. Those questions will be addressed to the ordinary citizen as well as to the public official.

From the above you can gather that sympathy is okay, but soft-headedness is not. The reporter is not an instrument of this philosophy or of that one. While he must measure what *is* against what *can be*, that comparison needs to be framed within the limitations of what is possible. In a perfect world, there would be no pain, no poverty, no unemployment, no sorrow. But the world is not perfect; neither are the people in it. The reporter's duty is to report on events and explain them, but in a manner that is sober and realistic. Very few issues are divided between the all-good side and the all-bad side. Rather there are likely to be two social goods in conflict, or two (or more) protagonists whose purposes, goals, and sense of mission differ. In dealing with people, the reporter needs to understand "where the person is coming from," and respect the fact that his worldview and values may differ fundamentally from the reporter's own. At the same time, the reporter should recognize that it is easier for an interviewee to make verbal attacks than it is to offer specific remedies, and good journalism requires that we move from the easy and superficial sound-bite to explanations of what alternatives there are, and what tradeoffs are necessary to effect change. A good television reporter will ask the person interviewed to confront the other side's problems and say how he would deal with them.

The reporter needs, as well, to probe the source of an interviewed person's anger or rage. Sometimes the target chosen may be the easy target, or the handy target, when in fact the individual may really just be angry at himself for not getting his act together. Plainly some judgment has to be made about the sources the reporter goes to in search of a story. There is a temptation, particularly in television news, to turn to the most articulate, the loudest voice, the most readily available person. The need for "good television" thus supersedes the demand for truth. Television often turns to the most militant, the most extreme voices, because these compellingly simplify and clarify the issues. The he-said-this, but she-said-that story intensifies and dramatizes;

but unless it is followed by explanation that reveals weaknesses and pitfalls and possible areas of compromise, it ends up substituting emotion for reason, and ill serves the public.

Sometimes you will come up against an individual who rails against "the system." Complaints against the system are usually so general, so amorphous, that it is hard to pin them down. Before you air that complaint, you need to ask the speaker to define "the system," and explain which part of it he thinks is unfair, and how *he* would do things if he had the chance. Never underestimate the power of a television interview to force the interviewee to see the holes in his case, or to examine the implications of his position. This works for ordinary citizens as it works for officials. Anyone who gains access to a television news program can be and should be expected to have thought through his position.

The reporter needs to have a sense of what is significant and central in a story, and lead the interviewee to a position where these matters are dealt with. It is too easy, especially in television, to accept the glib and colorful epidermis and leave untouched the muscle and bone. It is surprising what amazing riches can lie buried in the mind and heart of ordinary citizens, if only you ask. Studs Terkel's remarkable book, *Working*, is a valuable affirmation of this point. The thoughtful comments of steelworkers, waitresses, salesmen, and ordinary citizens from all walks of life, show what good journalism and intelligent interviewing can uncover. You should work to strip away the clichés, go behind the myths, and seek the patterns and the wider implications of the things you are being told.

One of the bonuses of being a journalist is that you are bound to get educated along the way. It is important to keep an open mind, and be willing to pursue information that you neither expected nor wanted to hear. Some reporters have preconceived ideas about who is the good guy and who is the bad guy and they thus fall into the trap of what *New York Times* columnist William Safire calls "a selectivity of interest in wrongdoing." What you get then is reporting that has a double standard: attacking those the reporter thinks unworthy, going easy on those the reporter considers on the side of God. In the process, the public is shortchanged, because it is getting only one version of the real world—the reporter's personal version. And that's definitely not what a fair press is all about.

CHAPTER FIFTEEN.

Writing for Television

Good writing is good writing whatever the medium. It can be recognized by its clarity, simplicity, precision, and color. However, television writing differs from print because the television writer aims to reach the listener and viewer instead of the reader.

A printed story can be read and reread. The reader sets his own pace, stopping to mull over a word or a phrase if it puzzles or intrigues him. In the spoken word of conversation, if you do not understand me, you can say, "I missed that. Will you repeat it please?" But in broadcasting, the viewer cannot stop the reporter in midstream and ask for clarification. Thus, writing for the ear demands that you say things in ways that the ear is able to absorb and that will not require repeating.

The style of broadcast writing is natural and conversational. It is less complex, less formal, than print writing style. Even though the reporter has to put his script down on paper, he is in fact *talking* into his typewriter. He is telling his story the way he would tell it to a friend or acquaintance, although not with the same personal opinions and embellishments. Television writing is a modern form of the old-fashioned storyteller's art, heightened by the addition of visuals.

Before you do any writing, your news director or program producer will ask you: "What do you have?" At that point you are expected to tell him, in simple, natural, lean prose, what the story is. If you have gathered your information well and have absorbed its meaning and its significance, you should be able to explain your story in a brief and intelligent fashion.

On the other hand, if your reporting is inadequate, or you are still confused about the import of the story, it is likely that you will respond to your boss with a garbled and confused answer. The story that subsequently emerges from your typewriter will be equally confused.

Before you talk with the boss, and before you try to do any writing—*think.* The thrust of the story should be shaped in your mind before you attempt to relate it to others.

Remember that the story is what it is in *journalistic* terms, not in terms of what visuals you happen to have captured with your camera. There is a temptation to tell the boss that the story you have is lively and colorful—"sexy," in newsroom jargon—when that explains little about the information gathered and its newsworthiness. Avoid this temptation. Stick to journalism. Communicate as a journalist who deals in ideas and information, and not like a theatrical filmmaker. You'll be treated with more respect if you do so.

From the above you can gather that the first act of writing for television is deciding what the story is about. This is your lead, and this is what you will write for the anchorperson. You can write a soft lead or a hard lead for the anchorperson, depending on how you intend to shape your video package.

The hard lead contains the most important information—what happened. The anchorperson who reports the hard lead then introduces you, the reporter. Your job is to provide supporting evidence, background, explanation, and counterbalancing viewpoints.

A soft lead has the anchorperson say something to tease or entice the viewer, and then lead to the reporter for the hard news.

Packaging the video story affects the television writing process because when you choose a sound-bite and pictures to voice-over, you are doing what a print reporter does when he decides which quotes to use, and where and how he wants to use them. The packaging also determines the overall shape and structure of the story. In one sense then, the process of determining the videotape package is electronic writing.

To repeat: how you plan to package your story will help you to decide how you write for the anchorperson, that is, whether a soft lead or a hard lead will best lead in to the package.

This Is an Example of a Soft Lead

ANCHOR O/C: Mayor Harvey made his long-expected announcement on the fate of his Deputy Mayor this afternoon. Robyn Smith has the details:

This Is an Example of a Hard Lead

ANCHOR O/C: After weeks of rumor and uncertainty, Mayor Harvey has asked Deputy Mayor Hildenbrand to resign. Robyn Smith reports:

In the soft lead, the anchorperson is trying to attract the attention of the viewer by saying, "Hey, here it is, the news we've all been waiting for." He then leaves it to the reporter to tell what the specifics of the story are.

In the hard lead, the anchorperson says in effect, "This is what happened," and he introduces the reporter to tell the hows, whys, and wherefores of that piece of news.

Whatever you write, whether it is for the anchorperson, for yourself on camera, or for your videotaped story, you need to remember some basic principles. Use mostly simple, declarative sentences. Tell us who did it, what he did, and to whom. Avoid long, tangled sentences that have a lot of dependent clauses. If you can break up information into reasonably short segments, you will be helping the viewer's mind to grab each piece and chew it before moving on to the next available information.

This is not to argue for writing that is so simplistic that it sounds like a "See Jane run" primer. Although your audience will be drawn from different educational levels, you simply cannot use this knowledge as an excuse to write copy for six-year-old minds. Simplicity and brevity do not preclude writing with liveliness and with a natural flow between one sentence and another.

Use words that are familiar to the ear. Some words are the kind that you would rarely hear spoken, and if spoken, they will startle and confuse. If you are writing a word that you don't know how to pronounce—because you've never *had* to pronounce it—you are wise to choose another, more familiar word in its place. There is a vocabulary that we use in talking, and at times it is quite different from what we use when we read and write.

In natural speech, we often use contractions. In formal writing, we generally do not. Write a series of sentences that include "is not," "do not," "will not" and then read these aloud. You will notice immediately how stiff they sound. In normal speech, we don't talk that way. Contractions are commonly used in broadcast writing. However care must be taken not to use them in ways that could confuse the listener. For example, there are times when "did not" is preferable to "didn't," because the contraction may be lost to the ear. For emphasis and for clarity, use contractions with care.

Broadcast writing differs from newspaper writing in a number of ways. The following is an example of a newspaper lead:

"As a result of severe budget cuts, the number of patrolmen hired by Middletown City dropped by fifteen percent last year, while reported crime increased by the same percentage, according to Roger Marion, Middletown City Police Commissioner."

Read those sentences out loud. You will notice that what works perfectly well in the print medium is less than satisfactory for the ear.

A listener would have trouble absorbing the information in the story because he does not know who is the source before he receives the information. By the time he finds out who is being quoted, he has missed key facts.

Remember that people often watch television while they are doing other things—preparing dinner, sewing, eating, even doing homework. A reasonable level of attentiveness and interest cannot be presumed. You have to structure your broadcast story in a way that will attract the viewer's undivided attention, and give him information in a form that he can grasp easily.

Thus for television, you might write this way:

"Anybody who lives in Middletown City, Iowa, knows that there have been a lot of muggings and robberies there recently. Now, Middletown Police Commissioner Roger Marion is saying that one reason crime is up is that the number of policemen hired last year went down. The police commissioner says that severe budget cuts forced the city to hire fifteen percent fewer policemen to patrol the streets, and reported crime went up by the same fifteen percent."

Notice that, for television, there is a soft sentence to open with—the kind of sentence that could be called a throwaway. Recognizing that the viewer may not be totally attentive, the writer here offers the throwaway as a means to attract the viewer's attention. He then goes on with the hard news.

Observe the way the different pieces of information are broken up, sentence by sentence. While the newspaper lead was contained in one sentence, the television story takes it in bites:

1. Sentence to attract listener: if you live in Middletown City, Iowa, you know how bad things are.

2. Sentence indicating source of story, and linking crime with the reduced number of police hirings.

3. Sentence indicating cause of reduced hirings, and the percentage of the drop.

Notice that in newspaper style, the information tends to come before the attribution. In broadcast style, you say who said it before you relate what he said. You also give an individual's title *before* his name, not after, and you strip that title down to its bare bones.

Notice, in the third sentence of the broadcast example, that the source of the story is repeated. This is intended to help viewers who may have missed identification of the source the first time around. However, this reidentification is more useful in copy or tell stories than when you are writing voice-over videotape. If the pictures show the police commissioner and his name comes up as a super (that is, lettering superimposed on the pictures), you can use the pronoun and leave re-identification to the visuals.

Observe the tense of the sentences. The present tense or the present perfect tense is often used for broadcasting, while past tense is the logical choice for newspapers. The newspaper reports events that happened yesterday. The broadcaster is talking today about events that happened today.

Furthermore, it is natural to use the present tense when we speak, even when we are talking about something that happened in the recent past. The viewer is in effect asking, "What's the news now?" and the reporter is answering, "The police commissioner is saying we have more crime because we have fewer police." The commissioner made his statement earlier that day, but the information is still timely, and thus it can be related in the present tense.

However, when you are writing a television lead, don't strain to put it in the present tense. If it feels more comfortable to use the past tense, do so. The above story could be written for broadcast this way:

"Middletown Police Commissioner Roger Marion said this morning that crime has increased in the city because the number of policemen hired last year declined." When you write the story in the past tense like this, you need to tell when it happened. You use "this morning," "this afternoon," "tonight," to indicate that, even though the event occurred in the past, it is still recent and immediate.

Even if you use the present tense in your lead, you are probably going to make the transition to the past when you begin to write your voice-over for videotape. It is plain to the viewer that the events you are showing on videotape occurred in the past, and you will have to tell the story that way. If your story is not tied to a specific event and is rather a "situation report" about a continuing story or a feature, you can use the present tense over videotape without a qualm.

The following are some pointers on writing news copy for television:

• Avoid dependent clauses. Where you have a long, complex sentence, break it into its components and make separate sentences.

• Don't overwrite. Keep it simple.

• Avoid unecessary adjectives and purple prose.

• Use the active voice. Say who did it, what he did, and to whom he did it. Use active, muscular, vivid verbs—but don't hype the story for the sake of color.

• Don't open your story with an unfamiliar name or a heavy dose of statistics. Ease into the story so that the viewer can absorb basic essentials before you hit him with the complex stuff.

• If you have to use a number, use it in round figures. Instead of "7,843,563," say "nearly eight million." Write numbers in words ("eight" instead of "8") to avoid trip-ups when you read the script.

• When you edit your script—and you should edit it carefully and ruthlessly—cross out *entire* words and retype or print them clearly above. If your script looks terribly sloppy, retype it so that you can read it without confusion.

• Abbreviations should be clearly marked out on your script, with hyphens between each letter: I-R-S, and F-B-I can easily be read without flubbing.

• Don't use middle names or middle initials. Keep it lean.

• Use the simple word instead of the literary one. Use "send" instead of "transmit," "cost" instead of "expense," and "large" instead of "massive."

• Make every word count. When you lead in to a sound-bite, don't repeat the phrases that will follow on the videotape.

• Avoid tongue-twisters, or phrases with a lot of hissing sibilants. Read your copy out loud to make sure that what looks right on the typewritten page sounds right to the ear.

• Don't be afraid to be eloquent, or colorful, to employ metaphor, humor, and other devices for the artful use of the English language.

• When you are typing your script, finish a complete sentence on the same page, and mark the bottom of the page with "(more)." If you jump a sentence to the next page, you risk on-air embarrassment if the pages happen to get out of order. At the end of the script, write xxx.

The television reporter may write brief lead-in copy for the anchorperson, but most of the time he is writing to pictures. This requires that he use his words with care and restraint.

Where you have fine visual material and lively sound-bites, you may be tempted to let the pictures make their point without undue interference from you. Don't be afraid to leave untouched segments of natural sound where this adds reality and mood to the story. On the other hand, you should avoid being intimidated by the visual, to the point where you are reluctant to explain what's going on. Television news—at least where it involves the coverage of news and not mood pieces or features—is rarely *cinéma vérité*. Your input and explanation are usually necessary to understanding, and you should not shrink from that duty because you have come back with lively pictures.

However, sometimes significant points can be made by the video alone, and when that happens you should allow the viewer to make the discovery himself. This will free you to make other, supplementary points in your voice-over. Remember that because each news story is brief, you must use each element, visual and aural, with economy and purpose.

When you are writing a voice-over, you should avoid conflicts between the visual and the aural. What you are saying while the pictures are seen should not conflict with what the viewer is watching. If you are reporting that the Mayor looked sad as he approached city hall, but the video editor has put in a picture of the Mayor smiling, you have an unnerving conflict between picture and words.

When the picture story is edited first, you will be expected to write your voice-over to match the pictures. In such cases, make sure you know what pictures are in the story before you write your script. However, in most television operations, the reporter records his script, and the pictures are laid over the sound. This latter procedure is the preferable one, because the editor can find pictures to match, or at least not contradict, the words, and the reporter is likely to be spared the embarrassment of saying one thing while his pictures say something else. Remember that, under the fierce deadline pressures of television news operations, problems have a way of cropping up, but if they can be avoided they should be.

One of the most common mistakes of the novice TV reporter is writing a script that tells the viewer what it is that he is seeing. The pictures show the Mayor laying a wreath at a policeman's gravesite, and the reporter is saying, "The Mayor then laid a wreath at Officer Meredith's grave." This video scene might best be left to itself, with natural sound or silence; or else the reporter may want to use the pictures as background to report the Mayor's determination to raise more money for bulletproof vests so that other policemen will not suffer Officer Meredith's fate. The pictures reveal the policeman's fate and the Mayor's concern, and the words voice-over take the story to its next level—what the Mayor intends to do about it.

Don't be afraid of simple, elegant, and eloquent language. The precise word, the telling phrase, the illuminative connection between what is seen and what it means can heighten the power of any television story. Vivid writing has its place in television news, but as with any other form of writing, the reporter has to put time and energy and imagination into it if he is to master the art. Too many reporters are content with the first plodding draft that pours out of their typewriters. As a result, many fine opportunities for creativity are lost.

CHAPTER SIXTEEN.

Planning the TV News Program

Television news programs used to be the stepsisters of local station operations. They were brief, they were understaffed, and they were run on a shoestring.

In recent years, station managements have discovered that television news can be a moneymaker. Local stations can garner between 50 and 80 percent of their profits from local news. As a result, managements that once perceived news as merely a dutiful fulfillment of the public service requirement of the Federal Communications Commission today give those news divisions devoted attention.

This development has its plus side. Programs are longer; reporters, staff and anchorpeople are better paid; and there is a large investment in up-to-date electronic equipment. It also has its minus side. Managements schooled in pure profit-making or entertainment concepts are injecting their values into the business of television journalism.

The television reporter is normally out in the field covering a story or back at the station supervising its editing. He is either writing or delivering the story on the air. He is involved in his small slice of the program's totality. However, his work is affected by the philosophy of the station's management, the inevitable struggles between that management and the news director, and the bottom line. The bottom line in the broadcast industry is ratings.

If it is to survive, the local news program must show evidence that it can attract large numbers of viewers and beat out the competition. Inevitably, this sets up an inner conflict between the concept of news as news—as *real* news—and the idea of news as entertainment. The mass of television viewers, who are accustomed to watching action film, conflict, emotion, and excitement in their entertainment programs, expect the same elements to be offered in commercial television news. If they do not get them from one news program, they tend to turn to another channel that gives them what they want; and where the viewers go, so go the advertiser dollars in hot pursuit.

Some critics, who in their own business operations would pale with fear if they saw red ink on their ledgers, do not mind chastising television news for doing what comes naturally in profit-making ventures, even those that are federally licensed. Follow the consumer, follow the advertiser, and follow the big buck are ideas as American as apple pie.

Television news is a marketable commodity, like peaches, computers, toothpaste, and refrigerators. So is news that is printed in a newspaper or a newsmagazine. If the advertisers and the readers do not like a newspaper or magazine, the operation is unlikely to survive, as the publishers of some big-city newspapers in particular have learned in recent years. In a free enterprise system like ours, the news "business" becomes just that. The alternative to that system is news by government fiat. What we have may be flawed and imperfect, but unless something better comes along, we have to make the best of it.

What does make news different from other commodities, however, is that it carries with it certain social responsibilities that are vital to the survival of a democratic society. The democratic compact between government and people will remain valid only as long as the people have some way of keeping watch on their government to make sure that it is neither incompetent, tyrannical, nor corrupt. The average citizen is too busy with his private life to have the time to do a private investigation of these matters. He expects the media to do it for him.

Thus, a television program billed as news bears a certain responsibility to provide news—real news, and not the ersatz kind. The ticklish problem facing the industry is how to inform on significant matters without at the same time losing viewers and income.

These built-in tensions—between profit and public service—continue to haunt television news operations as they do those in print and publishing. In addition, television news is relatively young. As a visual mass medium, it cannot draw on the history or traditions of print journalism alone to solve its problems. It has to carve out a viable and responsible value-system of its own.

The tug of war between journalistic imperatives and entertainment values goes on daily in local television newsrooms around the country. Sometimes one side wins. Sometimes another. Sometimes, the result is a melding of the two ideas into programs that manage to inform intelligently while delighting the eye and the ear.

A television producer once admitted to me that ninety percent of what he put on the air was "junk." But, he said, if he could produce ten percent quality news, he felt it was worthwhile. Some of those who shape local news programs are trying to improve that ratio, while others have succumbed to the imperatives of showbiz, and are pushing the other way.

It is against this background that the new reporter should come to understand how the evening newscast is shaped. Why did the producer decide to lead with a soft news story when there was a good hard one available? Why so much emphasis on crime and fires? Why was the reporter assigned to cover a minor hoopla in the city park instead of something more substantive? Why does the significant story on Councilman Jennings get a minute and a half of airtime while a sports story takes three or four minutes?

Time on television is often equated directly with space in print journalism, but the judgments about merit are based on different perceptions of what the medium demands. A serious newspaper will put an important story on the front page, even if the story is dry, filled with statistics, and there is no photograph to go along with it. The newspaper is fulfilling the expectation of its readers. Its editors believe that people buy that particular newspaper to find out what news is important, they expect the more important news to be on page one, and they expect that it will be dealt with in some depth. The story is likely to run many columns of inches, although it will be jumped to an inside page. Thus the serious, interested reader can find out what is important and then read the entire story, whereas the casually interested reader finds out what is important, and can then choose to read the headlines and the first and second paragraphs only.

However, the front page of a newspaper is not the equivalent of the top of a local television program. The television viewer wants to know what is important, too, but he will not necessarily sit still for a lengthy dissertation at the beginning of the program. There is no equivalent of the jump page in television. If the producer wants to lead with a particular story that is important but visually dull, he has one of three choices: he can go ahead with the dull story in depth and risk losing many of his viewers; he can tell the important story as a headline read by the anchorman and then move on to something more interesting visually; or he can lead with something less important but more lively, and hope in that way to grab the viewer's interest and entice him to remain with the rest of the program.

Unlike the newspaper reader, the television viewer cannot leaf through the total offering, choosing what interests him and ignoring the rest. Unlike the newspaper reader, he cannot choose to ignore the front page and read the comics and the sports section first—the way millions of Americans read their papers. He has to take his dose of television news as it is presented from the top on down. If he is turned off or bored by the opening story, if he is tired after a day's work and not quite ready for war, murder, inflation, and other bleak reports, he has only to turn the knob for relief. In order to exercise his freedom of choice, there is no need to get dressed, walk or drive to the local newsstand and plunk down a quarter for an alternative. The competition is readily available—free, at home, and at the twist of a knob.

Given that reality, television news operations have balked at the often-cited proposition that they should simply transfer the decision-making guidelines of newspaper journalism to their work. Interestingly, that proposition often springs from the writing of television critics, schooled in print journalism, who fail to completely understand the intrinsic differences between the two media.

The material for the evening broadcast is drawn from a variety of sources. First, there are the newswires. United Press International and Associated Press offer hundreds of news stories a day, ranging from local to state, national, and international. Then there are press releases from government and nongovernment organizations. Sometimes the stories that are covered by field reporters are follow-ups to the releases, or handouts, or follow-ups to stories in the morning or afternoon newspapers. Other sources of news are telephoned tips, telephone interviews, videotape from morning or noon news shows, material sent out by the networks on their syndicated feed, and of course tell and videotaped stories done that day by the station's reporters, or planned live reports with the minicam fed to the station via microwave.

Also available are special reports videotaped earlier, and reports from the weatherman, the sports reporter, the theater critic, the resident humorist, and assorted other beats like science and consumer affairs. Furthermore, as local programs have expanded from the original half hour to an hour and then two hours, live news interviews and feature interviews have been added to the mix.

With this smorgasbord spread out before him, how does the producer decide what goes into the program, what to leave out, how long each segment should be, and in what order the stories should be presented?

At this point it is important to remember that unlike any of its print relatives, a television news broadcast is a live event taking place in real time. The invention and development of minicams and mobile microwave equipment allow news events to take place in real time, not just the edited and condensed versions related after the fact. What this means to the program producer, at every level of his decision-making, is that the program should reflect a sense of "what *is* happening" and not just be a compendium of "what *has* happened."

Viewed in this light, immediacy gains in value and accounts for some story placements. It also makes news out of certain material, which if covered after the fact would be of minimal news value.

For example, impending changes in the weather can be important news on a six P.M. program, since the information, say, that the previously anticipated light snowstorm has intensified to blizzard proportions is of vital importance only if you know about it in time to make preparations. Similarly a news department may lead with a monumental traffic problem because for the audience watching the news in real time, that information is important at that point, though it may be of less significance five hours later on the 11 P.M. broadcast or the next day's paper.

The producer must also consider the placement of his local news program in relation to the national or network news. If his program goes on air before the network news, then he is likely to lead with major national and international events, since this will be the first opportunity for the viewer to be informed of those events. However, where the local program is preceded by the network news, the local program is likely to provide a strong local lead on the presumption that the viewer will already have seen the national and international stories. Local stations that are not affiliated with the major networks will provide a mixed program, leading with either local, national, or international stories, according to their importance.

The producer will also cast an eye on what is happening at competing stations. If he has the most popular sportscaster in town, he will run him at the time when the other stations put on their sports, in an effort to lure viewers over to his channel. The same approach is used in terms of scheduling the weather. Just as *Time* and *Newsweek* worry about each other's cover stories, and *The Washington Post* and *The New York Times* compete fiercely for the best front pages, so do local television stations when they are shaping their broadcasts.

Therefore, the producer looks at all of the material available, at the philosophy of the particular broadcast as well as the time the program is to go on the air, and he looks at what is happening at that particular time, and he starts to organize.

One factor that the producer must consider is the philosophy of the program. If the goal is to design a tabloid of the air, the producer will favor murders, rapes, fires, and gossip, and he will move that material swiftly and vividly across the screen.

If the program is more traditional, he will reach for the most significant story and, regardless of its cinematic merit, he will lead with that. He will follow up with other important stories and avoid catering exclusively to entertainment values.

Few local television stations produce news programs at either extreme. Most of them will include a bit of both philosophies, a mix of lively, interesting videotape and solid, straightforward news reporting. They will include some human interest stories and some with a humorous touch. They will respect the need to inform but not shrink from entertaining as well.

The resulting mix will depend upon several variables. The first determinant is how much actual airtime the producer has to work with. Several hours before the program is to air, he will receive a program log that shows him how many commercials will go into each hour. He then deducts commercial time from the total air time and emerges with a specific number of minutes to be filled by news.

The next variable is what happened that day, what the news is. For local stations, the newswires are the chief source of information about national and international events. For local news the producer will have a *news budget*, that is, a rundown of stories which are being covered by the station's reporters. Producers of the early evening news have been involved in the assignment process since early that morning and have a steadily clearer vision of the news program as the day goes along.

From all of this material, the producer must come to a decision about the most important story. However that is not necessarily the one with which he will choose to lead the program. He may instead opt for a story that a newspaper would report in one short paragraph on a back page, if it is reported at all. The story may be about a jolly baseball game in the local park, or how the city's people enjoyed the first sunny day after five wet summer weekends. Is this news? Of course it is. However, it is soft, feature, human-interest stuff, and not exactly what a thoughtful citizen would expect when he turns on his set to find out what is happening in his world.

By choosing to lead his program in this fashion, the producer is giving his viewer the impression that this, in fact, is the day's major story. That choice will reveal what news values are recognized by the management of Channel 2, or Channel 5, or 4. That first story puts its stamp on the entire program by indicating to the viewer the seriousness and professionalism of the people who are making the decisions. It will reflect the station's philosophy.

A more traditional, or if you prefer, serious, news organization will lead with the most significant story, even if it is in the form of copy read by the anchorman. The story may be brief, but it will be important.

Significantly, the choice of that lead story will help to determine the shape of the first block of the program. (A block is the segment of news stories between groups of commercials.) When the producer plans the block he makes every effort to link stories according to subject. If the lead story is about renewed warfare in the Middle East, the next story could be a report on the potential impact of the war on American oil prices, followed by a story on inflation, and then a feature showing how local people are dealing with inflation.

When shaping the news block, the producer plans for variety in presentation and in mood, with gradual shifts within the block. Videotape from the battlefront is followed by a montage of stills on oil prices, an on-camera report on inflation, and then a visually interesting and humanly appealing video story about ordinary citizens who are trying to save money. The mood shifts from the dramatic and the tense to the ordinary, but there is logic and sense as well as pacing in the way that the block is structured.

In some news operations, the next step is to decide how to end the program. Where possible, the producer will try to end the program with something light and upbeat. The idea is to persuade the viewer that things are not so bad after all, and to leave him feeling good about the world.

Between the two, the lead and the end-piece, a variety of stories will be packaged into blocks, or units. The modern producer tends to shy away from the old concept that the hard, unpleasant news should be put at the top of the program. He perceives that television viewers need relief from sorrow, suffering, pain and hate. A steady drumbeat of tragedy tends to leave the viewer weary and exhausted. Thus, in a series of waves, the program reaches a climax of shock and woe, then eases off for something light and unchallenging, and then later, it returns to stories that are murderous or scandalous or worse.

In his search for appropriate transitions from one subject to another, or one mood to another, the producer has to be careful that he does NOT saddle the anchorman with a juxtaposition that will be impossible to handle on the air. It is unfair to expect the anchorperson to move smoothly and credibly from a comic story to one that deals with death and disaster.

Producers often decide where to place a reporter's story, not just on the basis of its significance, but according to where it fits as a natural transition from another story, or according to its visual merits. If the show is bogged down with copy stories and the reporter has some lively footage, he may find his story moved up high in the program, even if it lacks major significance. If he has brought back a serious story without colorful footage, he may find it moved low down in the show where it can be appropriately separated from other heavy material. This is not the way that newspapers are structured. Nor do these principles apply as strongly at the network news level. But local news has its own perception of the viewer's needs, and its particular culture of decision-making. When criticized for judging news in this manner, those in local news are likely to respond with a smile and say, "I don't know. It works, doesn't it?"

These same principles are applied when the producer is deciding how long a particular story should be. The reporter who has lively and significant material will have to learn how to negotiate for more air time as well as for better billing. It will help him if he comes to the battle understanding some of the principles and pressures under which the producer operates.

CHAPTER SEVENTEEN.

Personnel in the Newsroom and the Field

By now you will have gained the impression that television news is a collaborative medium and that you will have to work closely with a number of people in order to get your job done. There is little room for the loner and the maverick in the television news business. The reporter has to deal productively with his co-workers both in the field and back at the station. There most certainly will be moments of high tension, and the deadlines are almost always demanding. The ability to appreciate and respect the labors of one's colleagues, even under pressure, is a valued trait for a reporter to acquire.

In the preceding chapter you learned about the crucial work performed by the producer or the executive producer of a news program. In other chapters you were told about the work of the field crews.

For the reporter, the most intimate working relationship will be with his camera crew. The reporter has to establish authority over the editorial content of the story and yet at the same time develop with crew members a sense of shared commitment to the excellence of the final story.

Unless you have a field producer to worry about such matters, it will be your job as the reporter to make sure that you have the appropriate shots and that the material is in usable condition. If you have any doubts about what you have, ask the technician to play back the videotape in the camera, and view it while you are out in the field. You can use an earpiece and watch the tape in the viewfinder if you have an ordinary camera. However many of the field videotape machines record, but do not play back, so a look is not possible. If you are working with a minicam and a van, you can review the tape on the monitor inside the van. Remember that, for a daily news story, it will probably be too late to reshoot material after you have returned to the station.

Both your camera operator and technician will be aware that one of the most common technical problems in field reporting is the failure of batteries used to operate the equipment. The reporter, too, should recognize the limitations of the batteries, which normally can record for only a half hour. Often the batteries give even less service than that in terms of optimum reliability, and pictures shot with a weak battery will suffer technically.

Recognizing these realities, when field producing you should try to arrange interviews for places where the equipment can be run from electrical outlets. If you must work away from the security of an electrical source, marshal your battery resources carefully, and don't ask the camera operator to overshoot.

This again points up how important it is for a reporter to understand the technology and to work within its bounds. The reporter who understands and respects the technical side of the business will be much appreciated by the camera operator and the technician.

In the last chapter, you were introduced to some of the responsibilities of the producer, sometimes called the executive producer, of the evening news program. At small stations, the producer may double as the news director or the assignment editor.

The news director is the overall head of the news department. He controls budgets, purchases major equipment, hires on-air talent and other personnel, and worries about the news product.

The effective news director has to exercise a rather special kind of judgment when he chooses the anchorpeople and the on-air reporters for his program. While he looks for star quality, attractiveness, good presence, warmth, and credibility in order to serve the visual requirements of the medium, he is also looking for individuals who are solid journalists and expert writers, individuals who can translate good journalism into the television medium.

In addition, it is the news director who hires the executive producer and the producers for different news programs. Because of the producer's intimate and daily involvement with the programs, this may be the single most important decision that the news director makes in determining the fate of his product.

When questions are raised about the ethics or advisability of going ahead with a particular story, or when crisis decisions have to be made, the executive producer normally turns over the problems to the news director. If there is a question of possible legal liability, the news director will turn to the station lawyer for advice.

While the producer shapes the program from the news material on hand, it is the assignment editor who decides which of many possible stories will be covered by local reporters. Several factors go into the decision-making process.

First, the assignment editor uses his familiarity with the particular talents and interests of his reporters to decide who will cover what. In most local news operations, almost all reporters are general assignment people, and therefore they can be assigned to any kind of story. But each reporter has his strengths and weaknesses. Some are more adept at breaking, hard-news events. Others can turn out eloquent prose-and-picture features. Still others have a flair for humor or investigative work. One reporter may be interested in social issues, while another is particularly knowledgeable about government. Wherever possible, the assignment editor tries to match the reporter with an appropriate assignment. However, sometimes he will be forced to employ instead the "nearest-warm-body principle," that is, he will have to assign whoever happens to be handy because there is no one else available.

Second, the assignment editor considers which stories are worth covering in any particular day. He will have on hand a list of local events from the AP and UPI daybooks. Unfortunately, many assignment editors lean heavily on these preplanned events because daybook stories offer the fairly secure knowledge that something will happen at a certain time in a certain place, and it will probably be usable on the air that evening. Enterprise stories, in which the reporter and camera crew go out on "spec" to find out what's going on, require an almost open-ended commitment of resources on a story that simply may not pan out. By playing it safe, in effect the editor is allowing the daybook to become the agenda-setter for the news operation. Where this happens on a regular basis, it is not the professional newsman who is deciding what is and what is not important or newsworthy. It is instead the government official or local activist who calls a news conference, makes a speech, or plans a demonstration. As a result of overreliance on daybook material, what the public comes to know is not necessarily what it wants or needs to know, but whatever the daybook decides they will know.

Some daybook events are, of course, worth covering. However, an effective assignment editor will check on the content and value of the story before he sends a reporter and crew to cover it. Sometimes the reporter is asked to make some preliminary phone calls and to report to the editor about the story's potential.

Other story ideas are drawn from news handouts. These are announcements by organizations or officials that a decision has been made or an event is about to take place. Most news organizations have what is called a *futures file* in which they place handouts about events that are scheduled for future dates.

A story may grow out of a report in the morning newspaper, or it can be a local angle to a national story that is moving on the wires. Some of the best stories are self-generated. That is, they spring from the interests, contacts, and imagination of intelligent and creative assignment editors, producers, and reporters.

In addition there are the stories that break suddenly and unexpectedly. The assignment editor is normally tuned in to the emergency radio channels for the police and fire departments, and these channels alert him to breaking events of that nature.

Third, the assignment editor has to consider the logistics involved in getting the reporter and the camera crew to the site of the story, and getting the story back and on the air. He needs to be familiar with his town or city and the outlying regions so that he can make reasonably accurate estimates of travel time. If an event is scheduled to begin at 10 A.M., and it is now 9:30, he will ask himself whether the crew can travel and set up in time, or is it likely that they will become bogged down in traffic and arrive too late? The assignment editor remains in contact with the crews and reporters in the field by means of two-way radio or telephone, and he is often expected to give directions or instructions on shortcuts to those who are heading toward a story. He will ask himself whether he should send the minicam truck and have the video signals beamed live back to the station, or should he arrange to have a tape picked up by courier? What other stories need to be covered, and can the crew members be moved efficiently to their next assignment? Is this particular story worth the investment of time and energy, or is there something equally good that is more easily obtainable?

These are among the many problems that confront the assignment editor. In many ways his job is different from that of the editor at a newspaper, since he has to concern himself so much with the technology. However, like the newspaper editor, his *top* priority is deciding what is news. He asks himself questions like these: Is this story substantive? Is it significant? Does the public have the right to know this? Does the public need to know this? And how can we arrange for the reporter to do his job well, responsibly, and in depth?

Many local television newsrooms seem understaffed, and this severely affects the work of the assignment editor. It is argued that because on-air reporters have garnered such high salaries in the television industry, many managements can afford to hire only a few of them. The expensive investment in personalities or "stars" limits the amount of money left over to spend on the necessary supporting staff—the researchers and young field producers who could double as reporter on routine and predictable assignments. Whether these are the true reasons for the shortage or not, the result is that some highly paid reporting talent is often assigned to cover minor stories because there are no junior reporters around to set them free to do more serious work. From the assignment editor's viewpoint the crucial imperative is to make sure that the air time is filled each night, the hungry television monster fed, so that the show can go on.

Finally, the assignment editor considers potential stories in terms of the visual requirements of the overall program. Most program producers are convinced that a program that is overloaded with talking heads will be dull, while one that contains too many insubstantial but visually attractive stories risks projecting the news program as lightweight and unserious. The producer will prevail upon the assignment editor to seek out some balance, to think of the needs of the final product.

For example, if the producer plans to lead the program with a major national story that will be read on camera by the anchorperson, the assignment editor may ask a reporter to do a visually interesting local angle to that story, one that could immediately follow the copy at the top of the show. Suppose that the lead story is the announcement of a federal cutback of Social Security benefits. The assignment editor could assign a reporter to interview local beneficiaries of Social Security and officials involved in the program to find out their perceptions of the consequences of the reduction in benefits. This story would fulfill the visual requirements of the medium and help to humanize the abstraction of the lead story, although the results of the interviews, in terms of substance, are likely to be predictable.

Some of the best television reporting is done on second-day and even later follow-up stories, where there is time to set up substantive interviews and to do some in-depth probing. A good assignment editor will encourage these projects because they add to the perspective and quality of the program.

Another key figure in the life of the television reporter is the associate producer, who is often a writer as well. Many local stations expect their reporters to package and write their own stories. However sometimes a reporter has covered a number of stories during the same day and one or two of those stories will be produced and written for narration by the anchorperson. It is the in-house associate producer who shapes these packages, with suggestions and input from the field reporter. The producer will determine the sound bites and instruct the editor as he puts the story together. He will then write the script for the anchor.

At the network level, field producers often go out with the reporters and crews and supervise the shooting and production of the stories. The presence of a field producer relieves the reporter of the need to worry about cover shots and the technical aspects of the story. It frees him to concentrate on his reporting and writing. However, the reporter must work closely with the field producer, sharing his perceptions of the story and its direction, so that the producer can obtain the material necessary for the final package.

The videotape editor is another key figure in the process of bringing an event from the outside world into the news program. In many news organizations today the cameraperson will also serve as the videotape editor. This procedure has advantages, because the cameraman knows exactly what shots he has on tape and he is already familiar with the material. However, he may be too close to the story to edit it objectively, and that can be a disadvantage. Furthermore, the fact that he is required to edit stories limits his availability as a camera operator.

Normally, the reporter either sends back written cutting instructions, or he returns to the station and sits with the editor to give verbal instructions as the story is being edited. The reporter should go into the editing room with an idea for the video package. But a good editor may see possibilities in terms of structure and continuity that the reporter has missed. The reporter should seriously consider suggestions from a creative editor, because a good editor can make the final story look both polished and interesting.

Once the story has been designed, the reporter writes his script. He should have in hand specific notes indicating how long the total story will be, how much he needs to write for voice-overs and lead-ins to sound-bites. Once the script is written, he records his narration by reading into a microphone that records his voice onto a videotape cassette. The editor then takes the tape of the reporter's voice and lays over it the rough video cuts that he and the reporter had decided upon earlier. He edits the pictures to fit the words and thus the final package is admirably synchronized.

One copy of the final program script goes to the director of the program. The director marks up the script to indicate which camera will be used if the story is to be delivered on camera, which tape machine needs to be rolled, what is the cue to roll, when to go to graphics, and so forth. During the live program, the director sits in the control room. He calls the camera shots to the camera operators on the studio floor, signals cues for tapes, for sound, and graphics, and he is responsible for the way that the final product looks on the air.

CHAPTER EIGHTEEN

What About the Future?

The technology of television is changing swiftly. The future promises development of a broad range of tools to make newsgathering easier and faster.

A few years ago, news operations worked with film instead of videotape. The film was expensive to use, becuase once exposed it could not be used again. Furthermore, since it had to be shipped back to the station to be processed before it could be edited, reporters had to complete their field work early enough to allow time for the processing to take place. The result was to limit the time available for field reporting and to delay the packaging of the final story.

The move away from film and toward the use of videotape is now nearly complete across the United States. Film is still used for some documentaries or for features which do not require prompt airing, but most stations cover the daily news electronically.

ENG makes it possible for the reporter to play back and review his visual material while he is still in the field, and if he is not satisfied with his stand-up or other material, he can reshoot it before he returns to the station. The minicams offer the option of using microwave technology to beam the live or videotape coverage directly back to the station, where the executive producer or assignment editor can review the story even as it is being shot. Ground stations (the minicam truck) can beam the story to helicopters which can, in turn, send stories from previously inaccessible places. Breaking stories that once would have to be reported on air by the anchorperson reading fifteen seconds of copy can now be presented by a reporter live from the scene.

New, more effective communications satellites make all of these processes easily applicable to stories that are breaking on the other side of the world. As the equipment grows smaller and more portable, shrinking technologies will make it possible to bring cameras into situations where the bulkiness of the old equipment would have prohibited access.

Plainly the new technologies are awesome. However, the central issue for journalists is how they can be used to improve the quality of the news product. That is, how can they be used to increase public awareness and understanding of significant events and ideas.

We have already observed the way that the live minicam can be employed either intelligently or foolishly, and the way that the visual demands of the medium can warp the reality which is reported. The culture of local television, built as it is on the economic imperatives of competition and survival, is being shaped by forces which are not always dedicated to serious and responsible public service. The new, more portable, global, and instant technologies offer no real answer to the question of what news is and how it best can be conveyed. Instead, they create an inner dynamic that shows preference for what is quick, easy, dramatic, and often trivial. Since the management has the technology in hand and vast sums of money have been invested in it, the technology is often used, regardless of content, in order to justify that investment. In the rush to employ the technology in this fashion, insignificant stories may be covered, while significant stories that require time for checking and cross-checking of information remain unreported.

What is happening in television news is related to technological developments elsewhere. We have evolved a culture dedicated to the idea of progress. If we have found out how to do something we go ahead and do it, and hang the consequences. In line with that thinking, we have built an industrial machine that has chewed up workers, required Madison Avenue to create appetites for nonessential goods, and poisoned the air, the earth, and the water. We have built nuclear power stations before we figured out how to remove radioactive waste. We built superhighways in order to serve millions of new automobile drivers, and thus opened the suburbs to swift development while nearly destroying the economic base of the cities.

If, on a larger social scale, we have done so many blind, willful and careless things in devotion to new technologies, why should we expect more restraint, wisdom, and consideration of consequences from managers in the television news business?

To answer that last question, the implications for our political system need to be considered. The premise that effective representative government requires an educated voting public remains as sound today as it did in the eighteenth century when the United States became independent from England. Today, when most citizens obtain their information about the world from television news, the quality of that news seriously can affect the nature and substance of public opinion.

There exists a real danger that the future of that news will be determined, not by serious journalistic imperatives, but by the gee-whiz nature of new technologies. The appearance of giving the news without in fact giving the news is like offering a meal that lacks the appropriate nutritive value. In the end, the viewer-citizen will suffer from information malnutrition.

Just as the reporter approaching a story needs to ask the right questions, so does the television news industry as it approaches the new technologies. The question now asked is this: how can we get the story faster, produce it slicker, and attract bigger audiences to our programs? A better question would be this one: What is it that the public has the need to know and the right to know in an increasingly complex and dangerous world, and how can the new TV technologies be marshaled to provide that information?

In meeting the high and serious purpose implied in the latter question, television news has to contend with what Christopher Lasch calls the "culture of narcissism," and which others have called the culture of hedonism and instant gratification. If the consumer of news, like the consumer of designer jeans or light beer, is interested only in a product that does not bore, but rather makes him feel good, then his tastes will be reflected in the news product offered on television. The marketers of news believe they are giving consumers what they want—action, entertainment, visually arresting material, and plenty of happy talk. On the whole, serious, substantive local news has not proved to attract the mass audience, and it is the mass audience that advertisers want to reach.

The future would look unrelievedly bleak if it were not for the fact that alternative news channels are now in the offing. Cable news, low-powered stations, and other communication channels will make it possible for some citizens to obtain their local news from additional sources. The rub here is that these new services require that the citizen pay for them, which means that those who cannot or will not pay must continue to subsist on the often inadequate diet of news offered by local broadcasters. What we will have as a result, is one segment of the population that has access to more and better information, while another one is fed pap. How that translates into decisions at the ballot box can only be surmised, but it is hardly a recipe for promoting intelligent democratic government.

The specific dangers in modern television technologies need to be considered before stations plunge ahead with a heavy investment in them. At least it would be wise to consider the journalistic risks, and to exercise restraint in the use of the technologies so that the risks are minimized.

• *Inaccuracy:* The public has the right to accurate, fair, balanced information. Public faith in journalism and the journalistic product rests on the belief that information that news organizations produce can be trusted. In the rush to go live, to be the first and the fastest, reporters cannot always properly check the facts in a story, and the risk of reporting inaccurate material is high.

• *Insignificance:* The public has the right to expect that what is called news is in fact news, and that it is significant enough to merit reporting either in print or on the air. The temptation in the new TV technologies is to cover stories that are dramatic and visually arresting, even when they have little real importance to the viewer.

• *Misshapen Reality:* In the search for visual excitement, the news tends to focus on visually lively exceptions to reality instead of the mundane but more representative rules. In order to humanize and to make a story come to life, television tends to use the dramatic paradigm, even where the example fails to represent the true situation fairly. In the search for what PBS correspondent Robert MacNeil calls "the right bit"—the lively sound-bite— some of the measured complexity of the truth is swept away.

• *Superficial:* The search for immediacy and visual drama often leads local news to present stories without appropriate explanation or backgrounding. Thus the viewer is bombarded with discrete bits of information and pictures, with little effort made to connect the information to other ideas and events, or to ground it in some historical background. The viewer learns what happened, but why or how it happened—the explanation so vital to understanding—is missing.

• *Manipulation by Sources:* Media-wise officials and citizens groups know that many news operations like to go live with breaking stories. As a result, the sources schedule their pseudo-events (news conferences, speeches, demonstrations) for the time when local news is on the air. An official announcement planned for 6.05 P.M. is likely to go live, unchallenged, and unedited, to the top of the evening news show. Furthermore, because of the timing of the "event," the reporter has no chance to follow the story immediately with a response from opposing viewpoints. Some news organizations are getting wise to this practice, and are refusing to cover such events live, but others continue to welcome the chance to show off their technologies and to put the viewer on the scene at a story as it is happening.

• *Crisis Journalism:* The best kind of journalism is the kind that digs under the surface of things and that forewarns the public about actions that are heading toward a crisis. This kind of journalism is the antithesis of live minicam reporting. It requires thought, preparation, research, and careful planning. It means doing many interviews, editing them carefully, and piecing together a story so that it makes a case. The new technologies discourage this kind of reporting. Instead, stories are reported when they reach crisis proportions and not before. Viewers are thrust into a dramatic crisis, but they come to it with little prior knowledge or preparation for understanding what led up to the situation. As a result, much public opinion is shaped in a climate of emergency, as a reaction to crisis, whereas long-term, considered, and knowledgeable opinion would be more constructive in shaping government response.

• *Degraded Caliber of Reporter:* The new technology gives to news directors greater incentive to hire reporters who are glib and can work live, even if the caliber of the reporting leaves much to be desired. While there can be no substitute for educated, thoughtful, perceptive, ethically grounded reporters to convey the news to the public, the tendency in TV news is to hire individuals whose talents as reporters take second place to their talents as performers or actors. The reporter who prefers patient and careful news-gathering and news-reporting methods, even though he lacks the moxie to report live on the air, is likely to be excluded in the future, and the consequent loss to the television news industry as well as the public will be tragic.

Plainly, television news, particularly local news, is engaged in an almost Faustian struggle for its soul. The tug of war between entertainment values and the values of serious journalism is tearing apart many of those engaged in the news business. The pressures from station managements to be first, to increase ratings, to jazz up the news product, work hand-in-hand with the pressures of the new technologies to present news that is quick, amusing and lively. Yet many of the people who are drawn to TV news are serious, engaged individuals who want to serve the public and to maintain high standards of journalism.

At a time when citizens must grapple with vital, complex, and urgent issues, and when they are turning in droves to television as their chief source of information, how the news directors, producers, reporters, and station managers resolve their problems has important ramifications for the society as a whole. Television news can either reflect reality or it can shape a universe warped and cracked like the reflection in a funhouse mirror. Citizens who view themselves in funhouse mirrors are hardly prepared to understand the real world, or to vote or act wisely and well.

Glossary

AIR-TIME: The hour at which the program is to go on the air. Also used to indicate the length of time allowed to a reporter for his news story.

AP: Associated Press newswire service.

A-ROLL: In film, the reel that carries the main picture and sound of the story.

BLOCK: The segment of a news program between two groups of commercials.

B-ROLL: In film, the secondary reel that usually carries silent pictures to overlay the A-roll material. Cutaways are usually on the B-roll.

BUDGET: Also called the News Budget. A list of news stories available to the producer for his program.

CAMERA OPERATOR: The individual responsible for physically shooting pictures in the field.

CHARM FACTOR: The risk that a reporter may lose his objectivity when faced with a charming and persuasive news source.

CINÉMA VÉRITÉ: Videotape or film shot in near-natural circumstances, with minimal intrusion or intervention by reporter or camera.

CUTAWAY: A shot that diverts attention from the main action although related to the story. A cutaway is often used to cover a jump cut or to give visual relief during a long segment.

DAYBOOK: An advance list of the day's events that runs on the Associated Press and United Press International newswires.

END-PIECE: The final story in a news program.

ENG: Electronic News Gathering. Videotape recording equipment and its related technology that allows for live reporting.

ESTABLISHING SHOT: A camera shot that puts the story scene in context by revealing background, atmosphere, relationships, or an overall view.

EXCLUSIVE: A story that is in the possession of one reporter only.

FCC: Federal Communications Commission. The Federal agency that licenses and exercises oversight of broadcast stations.

FIELD PRODUCER: The individual who is in charge of the photography, sound, and design of the news package during a field assignment.

FLAK: An officially designated spokesman. A public information or public relations officer.

FUTURES FILE: Sometimes called the tickle file. A collection of possible stories to be covered on specific dates in the future.

HALF-TRACK: Natural sound on videotape, with the volume lowered for on-air projection so that the newscaster can narrate (voice-over) while the sound is heard behind him.

HANDOUT: A news release sent by a government agency or private organization to media organizations.

INTERVIEWEE: The individual who is being interviewed.

JUMP CUT: The juxtaposition of one shot and another from the same scene with a resulting sudden jerky shift in the picture. A jump cut can be disguised by the overlay of a cutaway.

LAVALIER MIKE: A microphone that is attached to a cord and hung around the neck of the reporter. An additional microphone is worn by the interviewee. Lavalier mikes are used instead of a single, hand-held microphone.

LEAD: Usually, the first sentence of a news story. It is often written for the anchorperson.

LEAD-IN: The scripted portion of a news story that leads to another person on camera (anchor lead-in to reporter, for example) or to a portion of a videotaped story.

MAN-ON-THE-STREET: A random sampling of public opinion, usually taking place in a public area.

MINICAM: A portable videotape camera that makes it possible to deliver a story to the station live as it is occurring. Sometimes called an action-cam.

MORGUE: A library of clippings of already-published newspaper stories.

OC: On camera. Indicates that the reporter or anchorperson is live in the studio and seen on camera.

PACING: Internal development of the elements of a story so that the package holds the interest and attention of the viewer.

RAPPORT: A warm and respectful relationship between reporter and interviewee which improves the chances for an open and honest exchange.

REVERSE QUESTION: Also called A Reverse. A previously asked question that is repeated by the reporter after the original story has been recorded. The camera is moved away from its focus on the news source to capture the reporter's face as he repeats the question.

SLUG: The word or words used at the top of the script to identify the individual story.

SOT: Sound on Tape.

SOUND-BITE: A specific segment of a videotaped story that has been selected for use on the air.

STAKEOUT: In a stakeout, the reporter and camera crew set up outside of a developing event and wait there, with the hope that they can obtain an interview when the participants emerge.

STAND-UP: Videotape of the reporter on the scene, talking into the camera.

SUPER: (OR VF, FOR VIDEFONT): Words and numbers to be imposed onto the screen from the control room. A super usually identifies a speaker seen on the videotape.

TECHNICIAN: Sometimes called the sound technician. He is responsible for running the VCR and for the quality of the sound.

TELEPROMPTER: A device that allows the newscaster to read his script while looking directly into the camera in the studio.

TWO-SHOT: A picture that includes both the reporter and the news source. The two-shot can be used to set up the interview or as a cutaway.

UPI: United Press International newswire service.

VCR: Video Cassette Recorder. The equipment containing sound-and-picture recording machinery, attached to the camera by means of a cord.

VOICE-OVER (VO): Narration to be delivered as the videotape pictures are seen on the air. The voice-over can be prerecorded, or delivered live on the air.

VTR: Videotape recording.

WHISTLE-BLOWER: An individual, usually inside government or a private organization, who reports to the outside world privileged information he believes the public has the right to know. The technique often used by the whistle-blower is the leak.

WIND-SOCK: A cover for the microphone used in the field to minimize noise interference created by the wind.

Index

DATE DUE

DATE DUE			
NOV 0 4 1984			
DEC 3 0 1984			
DEC 0 7 1985			
NOV 1 6 1988			
JAN 1 8 1990			